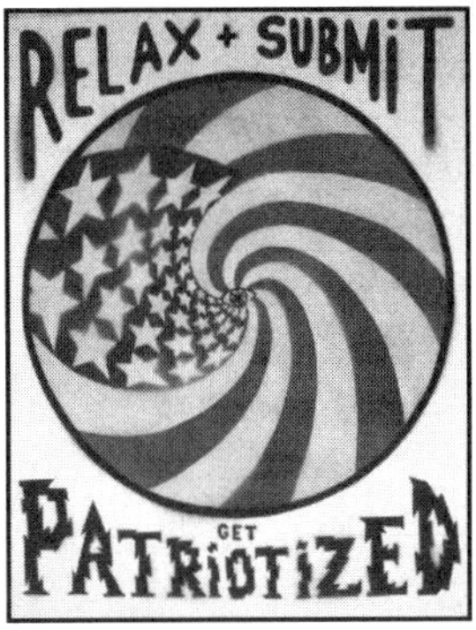

"Books and all forms of writing have always been objects of terror to those who seek to suppress truth."

— **Wole Soyinka**

All the days after

Critical voices in poetry and artwork

compiled by the
Upsidedown Culture Collective

UPSIDEDOWN CULTURE COLLECTIVE
DETROIT, MI

Upsidedown Culture Collective

Please get in touch with us:
P.O. Box 32780
Detroit, MI 48244
upsidedownculture@yahoo.com
www.upsidedownculture.org

Printed in the United States of America

Cover design and text by Upsidedown Culture Collective
Cover art: "Poets against the War" by Theodore A. Harris
Back cover art: "Gulf War Syndrome" by Nicholas Lampert
Frontispiece: "Get Patriotized" by David Loewenstein

ISBN 0-9741463-0-7
Library of Congress Control Number: 2003107777

Contents

Poetry

Illustrations

Seth Tobocman

Introduction to *All the Days After*

It has been over a year since September 11th, 2001. What has happened since then? It is a cliché to say that September 11th changed America.

But how have Americans changed? The conventional wisdom holds that the September 11th attacks would be followed by an all out endless war on terrorism in all its forms, pulling no punches, taking no prisoners, and with the enthusiastic support of all Americans and all right-thinking people around the world. But in fact, we have seen the largest peace movement in this country since the Vietnam War.

In the 1980s things were different. In the '80s it went like this:

The U.S. goes to war with a small third world country. There is no debate about this war because most Americans don't know the country exists.

The only Americans who seem to know about the war are those in the very small peace movement. The general population looks at the peace activists as being a bunch of wingnuts who have nothing better to do than worry about people in some country that no one ever heard of. This is only a slight exaggeration.

America has in fact had a very weird relationship to war. Our wars are never fought on our soil. The bombs fall in someone else's back yard.

Other people become collateral damage. Others lose members of their families or become refugees. World War 2 was good for the American economy, but it destroyed the economies of Europe. When Nixon got rid of the draft, war became worry-free for the American middle class.

But since September 11th, it is different. Now everyone has an opinion and everyone wants to know more about what is going on. When I get onto a subway train with a peace placard, everyone starts talking, the whole subway car wants to debate the war, and the split is about 50-50 for and against. These are dangerous times, but these are hopeful times.

Americans are awake and looking for answers. We must join in this debate. The voices of war have spoken. And now the voices of peace must be heard.

Seth Tobocman is an artist and political activist from New York City. In 1979, he began publishing the political comics journal World War 3

Illustrated *with fellow artist Peter Kuper. His comic artwork reflects his many years of involvement in struggles around police brutality, squatter's rights, corporate globalization and U.S. foreign and domestic policy. He has authored three books,* War in the Neighborhood *(Autonomedia, 1999),* You Don't Have to Fuck People Over to Survive *(Soft Skull, 1999) and* Portraits of Israelis and Palestinians *(Soft Skull, 2003).*

Roxanne Dunbar-Ortiz

Foreword for *All the Days After*

The September 11, 2001 attacks on the symbols of US military and economic might have revived the waning template of the country's origin story, a narrative of righteous settlers in the wilderness surrounded by murderous savages. The very establishment of the United States employed that powerful mythology, founding an empire for security, having to extend the boundaries of protection until they included the whole world, an imperialism for sure, but an imperialism of a particular and peculiar variety, and insanely dangerous for the future of humanity and the planet itself.

In the United States, monuments and histories that tell the story of white settlement and a "god-given" covenant between European Calvinist settlers and the land they "conquered" remain the scaffolding of the official national origin story. Although contested, the official story remains intact.

Despite all the fissures provoked by 60s and post-60s dissident thinkers, the ideological hegemony of Americanism has not been shaken. Antonio Gramsci conceptualized such hegemony as the complete and total domination of individuals to the point that no overt force is necessary to maintain control. Instead, capitulation to the dominant system appears consensual. It does not appear as domination at all, but perniciously, as common sense. The power of myth, Roland Barthes said, lies in its recurrence, making its historical contingency appear as eternal fact and enabling it to appear apolitical rather than historically and politically constituted. And George Orwell rightly pointed out that whoever owns the past owns the future and that those in power in the present control the memory of the past.

So what? The elite created a new reality for themselves in establishing the country. This has been true all over the world in the founding of modern states. But what is different here is not the historical behavior, but rather the denial or rationalization of it in order to continue the mythology of the origin of the United States. Until we are able to question and examine the origin myth, we will not be able to comprehend and eradicate the white supremacist and patriarchal bedrock of our culture.

U.S. historians are trained to be the keepers of the secrets and protectors of the myth. Since the cultural upheavals of the 1960s and subsequent demands for some kind of re-telling of the story, historians who guard the origin myth have countered with calls for "objectivity" and "fairness" in revising interpretations of U.S. history. They warn against "moralizing," calling for a dispassionate and culturally relative approach. However, when mass land appropriation and looting, murder and greed are masked in platitudes about a time of "cultural change" and "conflict of cultures," fundamental questions about the nature of the formation of the U.S. may be avoided. One historian, Bernard Sheehan, put it succinctly in a 1969 essay, arguing that an understanding of cultural conflict "diffuses the locus of guilt." Indeed it does. Furthermore, present responsibility toward that past can be rejected.

During the "American War," as the Vietnamese call it, the resistance fighters used to tell us that that the struggle for freedom is precious and that it would take a long time, that they regarded the American War as only a marker in their thousand year struggle for freedom and independence, that they struggled from one generation to the next. I've heard the Mayan freedom fighters from Guatemala and Chiapas express the same sentiment. But both the Mayan and the Vietnamese freedom fighters have got their history straight and clear.

In the United States, we haven't even begun to extricate ourselves from the pseudo-history of freedom that we still use as a point of departure. The savvy Egyptian writer, Samir Amin, in his Eurocentrism, puzzles over the difficulty that citizens of the North Atlantic states, including leftists, have in detaching themselves from a patriotism that validates historical colonialism, slavery, and genocide, as well as inherent contemporary white supremacy, under the guise of spreading the benefits and knowledge of "western civilization." Specifically U.S. citizens, including dissidents, cling to our origin story of a brave democracy gone awry, proposing strategies for "regaining" the "original intent," or for "taking back our democracy," in the words of Ralph Nader.

Sometimes it appears that the litany of U.S. historical crimes and errors only serve to strengthen the origin story, and the idea of loss of purity, loss of innocence, with a passion to regain it.

The left/liberal intellectual community espouses a sort of post New Deal nostalgia that identifies the "national security state" as the thief of U.S. democracy. This obviously is a Eurocentric perspective—and ahistoric—that ignores the hard-won gains of African-Americans, Mexicans, Native Americans, immigrants, women, and gays during that same period since World War

II. Such a perspective not only protects the origin story but also reinforces it.

Unfortunately, much of the African-American intellectual sector, as well as other oppressed groups, embrace a parallel analysis that, perhaps unintentionally, preserves the origin myth: the long road to freedom that began with an incomplete and imperfect Declaration of Independence that declared, "all men are created equal..." In the long struggle for freedom, women, those without property, immigrants, workers, women, struggled for inclusion in the original ideal.

However, both the tidy and the untidy versions of the origin myth stumble on its own contradictions when the land itself is considered. Woody Guthrie's national anthem, "This land is your land, this land is my land..." is as fallacious as "The Star Spangled Banner" or "God Bless America." Stolen land and genocide must be forgotten in order for the origin myth of "America" to function. Manifest destiny must rule the historical memory for the myth to survive.

Most U.S. citizens don't think of the their country at its founding as thirteen small colonies clinging to a small part of the North Atlantic shore, but rather the continental expanse from ocean to ocean— "from sea to shining sea"—and from Canada to what was until the 1840s the middle of México, the Río Grande. We must acknowledge how that transition happened. In fact, the elimination of the Native occupants of the land was necessary for the workings of the U.S. Constitution itself. African slavery was crucial for the accumulation of capital, but not necessary for the United States "republic for empire," as Thomas Jefferson put it; getting rid of the Native Americans was necessary.

Genocide is the subtext of the Constitution and its machinery. And a byproduct of both the genocide and the maintenance of African slavery was the integration of white supremacy (and Christianity) into the republican project.

Furthermore, there are no borders to America's destiny; long before 1898, the year that U.S. historians cite as a moment of aberrant U.S. imperialism when it annexed the Philippines and Puerto Rica, the Marine's marching song had been penned, "...From the halls of Montezuma [Mexican war, 1846-48] to the shores of Tripoli [Barbary Coast wars against North Africans during Jefferson's presidency]..."

Shock and Awe. That's the name of the 2003 USA genocidal campaign, this time against Arabs, still using Custer's 7th Calvary division as the "scouts," operating "Kiowa" death equipment and "Tomahawk" cruise missiles. At the end of the genocide, wiping up the blood in "Indian Country," a US military term of trade meaning "inside enemy lines," are the armored tanks division that traces its origins to the early 19th century genocidal wars against the Seminole nation in Florida. The Associated Press reported on March 19, at the onset of the invasion, that the armored regiment performed a "Seminole Indian war dance" before crossing into Iraq.

To those who admonish us that we must be patriots in our opposition, that indeed we are the "real" patriots, I say, "Not me, Babe, no, no, no, it ain't me, babe..." (Dylan). I am a proud anti-American, if "american" here refers to the United States of America.

Acknowledgement and disclosure of the "American" origin myth to the world, and to ourselves, is absolutely essential in order for us to develop a strategy to defang and neutralize the United States. Art, and particularly poetry, is the appropriate place to begin. This volume contributes to the process.

Roxanne Dunbar-Ortiz is a life-long political activist and one of the founders of the Women's Liberation Movement in 1968. She holds a doctorate in History and has been a professor of Ethnic Studies and Women's Studies at California State University, Hayward, since 1974. During that time, she has also developed specialization in the international law of human rights, lobbying the United Nations system for the rights of indigenous peoples, migrant workers, refugees, and women. Most recently, she has been writing and publishing historical memoir: Red Dirt: Growing Up Okie *(Verso, 1997),* Outlaw Woman: A Memoir of the War Years, 1960-1975 *(City Lights, 2002)* and Norther: Re-Covering the US Contra War in Nicaragua *(South End, 2004).*

Acknowledgements

Obviously, such an ambitious project could never be accomplished by such complete neophytes without a lot of help from a lot of people. So please excuse us if we forget anyone... First of all, many thanks to everyone who helped us raise the necessary funds to publish this collection. We enlisted many a performer's services to make our cabaret fundraisers happen. Thank you especially to Audra Kubat (your graciousness & eagerness to help really lifted our spirits), the ever-enthusiastic Maurice Greenia & his comrades in the Space Band & the Don't Look Now Jug Band, the fabulous Blair, Mick Vranich, Angela Jones, the Foreheads, F.I.A.S.C.O., Joanne Riedl, Ron Allen, David Watson & of course, to our ridiculous recruits who participated in wrestling & magic skits, of course also thanks to the Matrix Theatre & Trumbullplex for hosting us. & of course also plus, above all else, everyone who showed up, clapped & hooted—who really made it happen. Also, much gratitude is owed to everyone who donated work for our cheap art auctions, which not only helped to raise funds but helped spread the idea that art is not something reserved for the rich & the culturally elite. So thanks to Josh MacPhee, Claude Moller, Icky Apparatus, Merrydeath Stern, Bec Young, Collin Matthies & Connie McKinney. Thanks to Rad.Art in Ann Arbor for hosting us & helping us along on our common path. We want to thank all of our wonderful contributors. Thanks to Seth Tobocman for his wonderful introduction. Special thanks to Roxanne Dunbar-Ortiz for being so helpful & willing & wise, & Theodore Harris for going the extra mile & not only contributing his amazing collage art but also soliciting other contributors for us & just being an all-around swell guy. None of this would have been conceivable without all of the people who've made up Upsidedown Culture Collcctive at various points who, for whatever reason, had to move on. So Alma, Frank, Kime, Marie, Muhammad—we owe it all to you—thanks.

Angela Jones

Dig

There are forgotten truths in this soil
And I'm going to dig for them
But don't give me those tools that my brother used
To extract diamonds from a land that they once called home
Oh, no
See, I'm going to use my hands

I'll scratch with my nails and punch with my fists
Shaking the earth with their urgent blows
Until I hit some solid surface
The surface is a revelation so true
It's too true to bear witness to
            These violent secrets unveiled
Dirty like dust on my knuckles
That are angry and clenched in a fretful pose

This earth is not a lake
Where I can dip my palms in
And let drops drip from my fingertips
No, these secrets are too painful
            And the earth is unwilling

So I will make my hand of metal!
Digging through the cracked cement to excavate skyscrapers
Finding tombs of wombs
That bear the fruit of the privileged elite
            In moth eaten purple pin-stripe

My destiny is to dig for doubtless truths
Shattering dogmas with jackhammers
Hiding jailhouse files in my raised fist
To file away the bars of steel mines and copper mines
Freeing ancestors of mine and yours

From slavery, indentured servitude, and minimum wage

This earth that hides the headlines and hell raisers
Of old revolutions
Is the same that bore me into
A kingdom of corrupt kings and cruel intentions
This institution is not amorous
It knows its sins
        Now I shall know them, too

This dirt is soaked with nuclear test sites
Ghetto mounds of grass-covered garbage
Where children run through mutated weeds
The dirt is carried into the wind
Gets in your eyes and blinds you from
The internment camps that were once there
In this soil rests the sullen graves of adobe huts
And in their place grow reservation HUD houses
        And welfare cheese

Barrio booze and CIA-sold street crystals
All picked from the same genetically engineered tree
Grown in the closet we bury our skeletons in

The deep, dark depths of earth
Hide the secrets to shame and bad decisions
What's fair isn't often forgotten
And freedom isn't found from a flag
        You have to dig for it

So dig for your freedom
Fragile figures of history's failures
Or I'll dig for you
For those fools of fortune

I'll plough through the lies and muck of middle-earth
And turn stock shares into plough shares

Giving the campesinos back their polycultural crops
I'll worm my way through the holes in this planet
To other kingdoms and freedoms forgotten
            Because this earth is not rotten
It cleanses itself every other empire
By hands that dig for the truth
Through the ashes of old tragedies and fallen legacies
We must keep the past in mind and at hand
            To seize the chance to begin anew

DIG

Jas

EPOCH

It's a matter of convenience
In the manner of consensus
With real force any age
Can become an epoch
The necessary time
For one's noise
To find measure of music
Requiring careful talk of
This and that
Rights and wrongs
But when it came
It came harder
Than we had ever guessed

Amiri Baraka

Fashion this, from the Irony
Of the world.

That I, the undaunted Laureate of the place, daunted in some
Un as yet/ed pre tense of what they see, they be
As if, such where they was
Was yet to be, and then to say
They is, and is not, like revelations, wow!
Humans. The skin, the lodging inside dumbness a slight breeze
frees they speech
To speak as if acquainted with small things in the world. Eating,
Belching, Farting, Murder, Robbery.
And so. As if, and them too they is. But nothing further
But the wee dots on the deletion resembling the minds of them
Yet to come.

Imagine you were me, or imagine you were thee
And we knew all the things both do. And is. And will ourselves
To be. Imagine you were in this place, and they wanted to run
everywhere pointless endless understanding not even why
They smell or they hair fall out, or what to do about
Gout. That they are yet stupid to colds and cancer and death-
They think holy
And ultimate. When death is simply a report card
Of the ignorant. Nothing dies but that which never lived
And it might return in a white suit and in charge of ugly small mistakes
Somebody at Harvard could win a billion dollars and a post
If they cd find out but they never will because it is the reason
They committed suicide

Suppose you had to live with
Ignorant white people and negroes
In cages, with important chains
Around they mouths. Suppose you
Had heard of Trent Lott. Suppose, you woke up one a.m.
And there was a vampire on the tube
Being interviewed by a Niggalino boob

A handsome rat, for whom the idea of brain
Was only an idea, which he did not think if he could
Was a bad one. And the boob was a killer yet to graduate
From killer school so he worshipped the vampire's teeth,
The two juicy fangs hanging from each end of his lip,
The negro thought was hip. And dreamed of having
Teefs like that so he could be a rat, he was tired of being
A mere heel. And the vampire was planning to bite the whole
World. To suck the blood out of everything. To suck the blood
Out of the world and make its future a vampire, that could whirl though
Space and suck the blood out of the stars, suck the blood out of the planets
Suck the blood out of the moon, suck the blood out of the sun
And then, armed and blubbery fat with everything's blood, still hot
And musical like emptiness, he could lift into the outer waygonesphere
And search for God, if there was such, and suck the blood out
of Him, Her, It, Them Whatever, till there was no Blood anywhere,
not even you, Blood, in fact
You be one of the first to go.

It was a special issue of Jungle Comics, where the vampire the
thin nosed kind
From the out back, who can suck with his teef and stir with
his nose, who eyes
Are missing, and what you see is the bottom of a cold mine
filled with 2000 fathoms
Of Lynch, Execution, Missing, Rape, Cheated, Framed, Slandered,
Stolen, Frown frozen ex corpuscles, hid under the glistening listening
underwater ASSCRAFT of the Satanic moron cult, whose breath
is toxic and pokes holes in the sky so dead things
Can shit on our food.

He is called Fonnghool the asshole, and dances to dry lips set on
fire by missing junkies he has eaten. He is the devil's newspaper
and wears his ass backwards so the colon can
Wear a uniform. And Revelations can be burned especially 18:12 where it
say beware of ugly mother fuckers who is not really ugly mother fuckers
but uglier much , much, much more uglier dan dat! So spake Nat! Amen.

I speak with the rage of Angels

Them that be with Marx.
I speak with the clarity and inferno of the necessary
Like my man John on Patmos watching skyvision and
Digging it was all commercials.

I speak like Ali Baba, ("The Arabian Pope")
who when he spoke the magic words,
"Open this sucker up", and the mountain swang, envisioned one day
There would be a John named Trane who would blow the same shit

I blow with the deep fear of John on the island looking at the actual devil
I am like him in that I try to count the mammyjammers heads and horns
And find out what will kill him.

I speak like him who spoke to Philadelphia and hung out with Jesus
Before they murdered him. I speak like him who dug that Peter
Was a coward and gave the Lord up, and that Paul was an Anti-Semite
Who never came out the closet.

I speak as one who knew Judas would drop a dime on the Movement
And confirmed the chump had hung his lousy self just before I got busted.

I speak as one betrayed by the lies of those who say they are religious but
Are greed ridden worshippers of Satan, who kill any one who opposes them
and calls it a church of Defense against Evil.

Like John, I wd speak, like the John who baptized, like John
the knower, John,
The Blower. John the Brown and John The Revelator. I speak like
James the Brother, James the other, Jim the hip, like Dick the
Rude, like Bird the high, like Monk the Deep I speak from the
island of my soul, and cast a terrified look into the sky filled with
monsters, with witches and devils with Great Whores and Beasts, of
things with heads and horns and blood dripping out of their eyes.

It is out, imagine, you were here, in this place, staring into the
soul of something
Filthy, trying to keep it from murdering you, to keep your eyes
from registering

Your ears from hearing, your mouth from reporting. And you could
feel it breathing on your neck and saw sometimes the shadow of its
horny hands reaching out of the
Blind dark you cd see the shadow of its gun its lie its teeth
sweating. Imagine you could actually understand its obscene ideas,
and they made you enter the mind of Fred Douglass And stare out
at the ocean just as John at the edge of Africa, staring at the
Overhead commercials on the death of the Beast.

And so the blessing that is in my name and in my words, I give to myself
And you who are truthful as the actual life of the world. And
it is this blessing
Which will save us, will make us strong, as we go on with our
work of scientifically
Determining how to kill the beast. Each night I fill my notebooks
with formula
And instructions to myself and others on what to do of what
to study of where to
Go who to talk to and when. I make lists of words, names, events, pro-
cesses, necessary stages of what we have come to realize is protracted.
And what we do we will do.
And what we succeed at, is worth the pain, what we fail at,
is worth the understanding if we can understand. What the next
step is. We are studying with all our minds and hearts and souls'
determination to understand how to slay the serpent. This task
Nat handed down to whoever did understand that that was what
he did, hanging on
That tree. Slain by the Serpent's hosts.

So we have learned that we can not die except by our own submission to it.
And have decided we will not die except when we understand
what place we go to.
And so begin to set that where in order and begin to understand
where the beast
Will be hiding there. We are the Rider of The Black Horse. Black
Horse Black
Rider, who conquers with a scale. With Justice and Measure and the
mighty pentatonic mode of the finite music of infinity, a new joint

And when I returned from this forwarding of my feeling and knowing
The beast sat still and teeth wiggled with lies and at once I remembered where
Before I'd seen him, before his tenure as the Counterfeit Ghost
of The Caucasian Crib. Yes, it was the same one. Remember the little
Devil Gerald 2X arrested and placed in the pages of Muhammad Speaks
And we saw him where Malcolm had locked him up, with the little
Horns out his head the evil eyes and the twin fang straws for
sucking oil and blood.

It got clear to me as he rose to leave, and the negro boob slobbered happiness
At being recognized as the newest commode in the Caucasian abode, the vampire
Turned and where before the cunning little tail that used to dangle out his hiney
Struck me at its absence, Oh, I thought, and at that moment I saw the thing dart
Like a copper head's fart out of the negroes curled lips, ringed with the white chalk
Caucasian Circle of Merit which identifies Wooden Negroes promoted
to the honorary genus of Homo Locus Subsidere (Literally, "Near
Man"), who no longer kneel when they are made well paid heels,
but now can assume the funky bedbug crouch of the
Hideously self hating. At the same time, they are given a grey facsimile carte blanche
Weapon of Ugliness to use against N words and any who wd violate the sanctity
Of northern appetite! And so I came to understand that the beast's deadly arrow,
Shot from out the lst horseman's white bow, from the white horse,
the weapon which Revelations prophesied to John, was the weapon
of his transitory rule, was now
The tongue of the boob, whom I err at calling him that, or rat, or heel, or dog, or
Traitor. That tail become a tongue was the sign, that from the vampire's tail
Was bestowed on the wooden negro a badge that allowed him to enter Klan meetings,
Skin Head Lynchings, Texas Executions, Palestinian Ethnic Cleansings,

and report
With the slobber of his terrificatious white ringed serpents beak,
symbol, font & punctuation on the tabula rasa of the media sheet
the empty echo of his eviscerated
Self, and in the soul's place that beast's tail was hung that beast's
tale was sung.
And I stood, remembering Patmos, and the images that sailed across the air
When you and I was there. And wondered what next the world
of this life held for those
Who would love goodness.

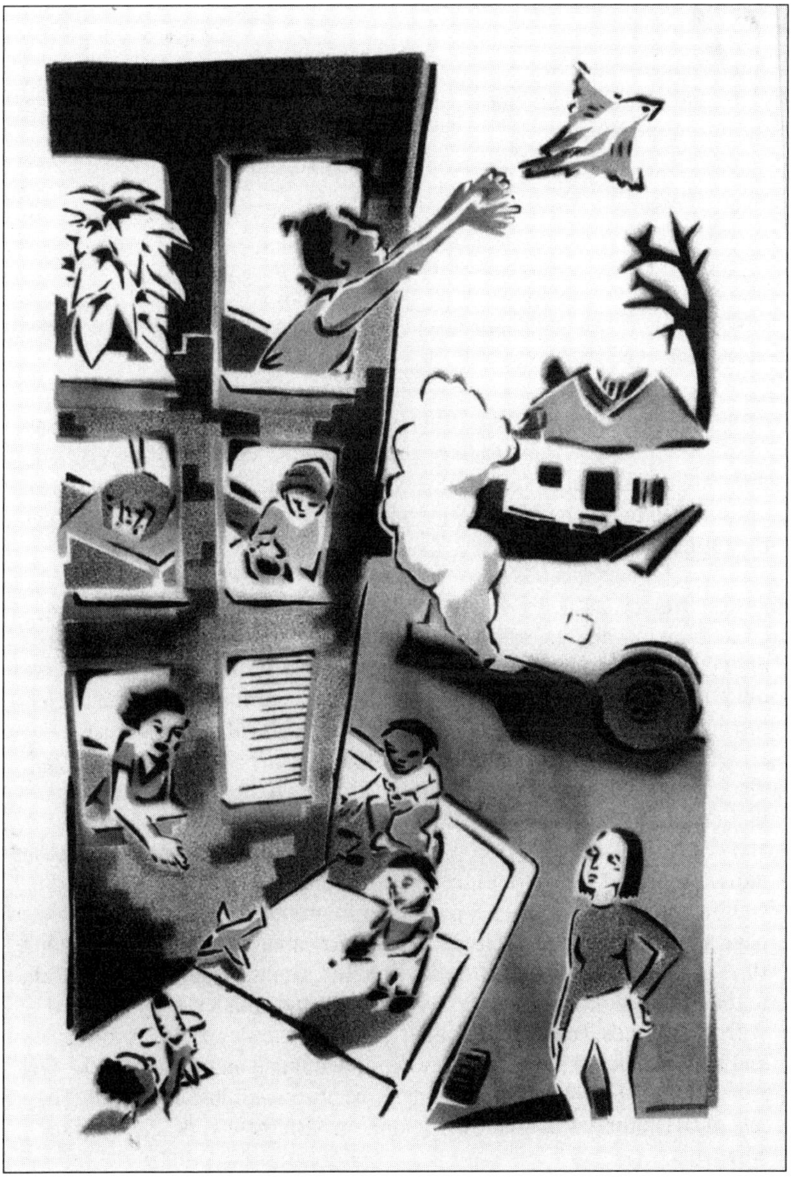

The scene of the crime
clues and (yes) beyond clues
the absence of lives
and so much debris (and smashed-up pieces), cleared
sad tourists
workers
photo-snaps
talk to strangers. The holes in the green-covered windwall
cut open for views and patched up again. people enter and surround the site.
What happened here last year?

From now on, the sky will hide black eagles in the chambers of its clouds (more to remember, more to hide, more to find). People will carry a new different sort of weight, as they wander through their lives. (yet, always returning to the scene of the crime so puzzled, angry, searching to change the future) ...

September 11, 2001
Quiet blue morning (sun-light) New York City (seems like so many other days) then—all hell breaks loose, stabbed in the heart, gut-kicked, everything upside down (the violence, the hatred, the chaos). Thousands gone, just like that, a day of loss. fire screams, things fly, blood, ash, dust, crumbling, explosions, crashings (a hole in the city). Out on the ferry, a black cloud, staring into the water. In Chinatown they shake their heads in disbelief. Up in Harlem a wail goes up for lost loves—lost brothers and sisters. In Central Park people sit on the grass, on benches, on rocks, radios tuned or talking. In Times Square, someone's crying with pigeons walking around her feet—people gather in groups. In the subways, most have someone they know. Someone to worry about. In the Village, people stare at an ugly grey hole in the skyline. In Queens, people are angry-talking to their televisions. In Brooklyn, some walk and wander—all shattered—with hung heads. In the Bronx, they gather on the stoops, in store-fronts and talk in shock & disbelief. New York, wounded and under attack—yet strong. Why? How? Sense of Safety & security—all lost and spent. The rest of the country (and the world) look on. (But new york, New york, New york....)

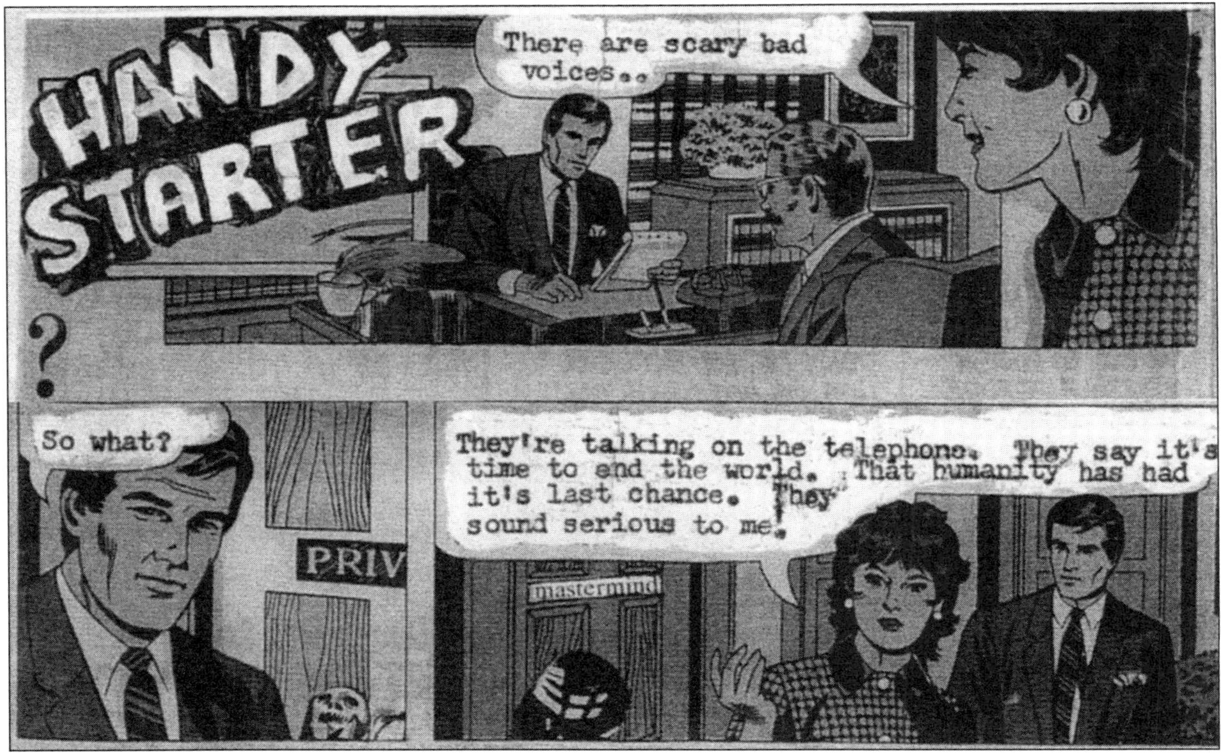
HANDY STARTER
?
There are scary bad voices..
So what?
They're talking on the telephone. They say it's time to end the world. That humanity has had it's last chance. They sound serious to me!
PRIV
mastermind

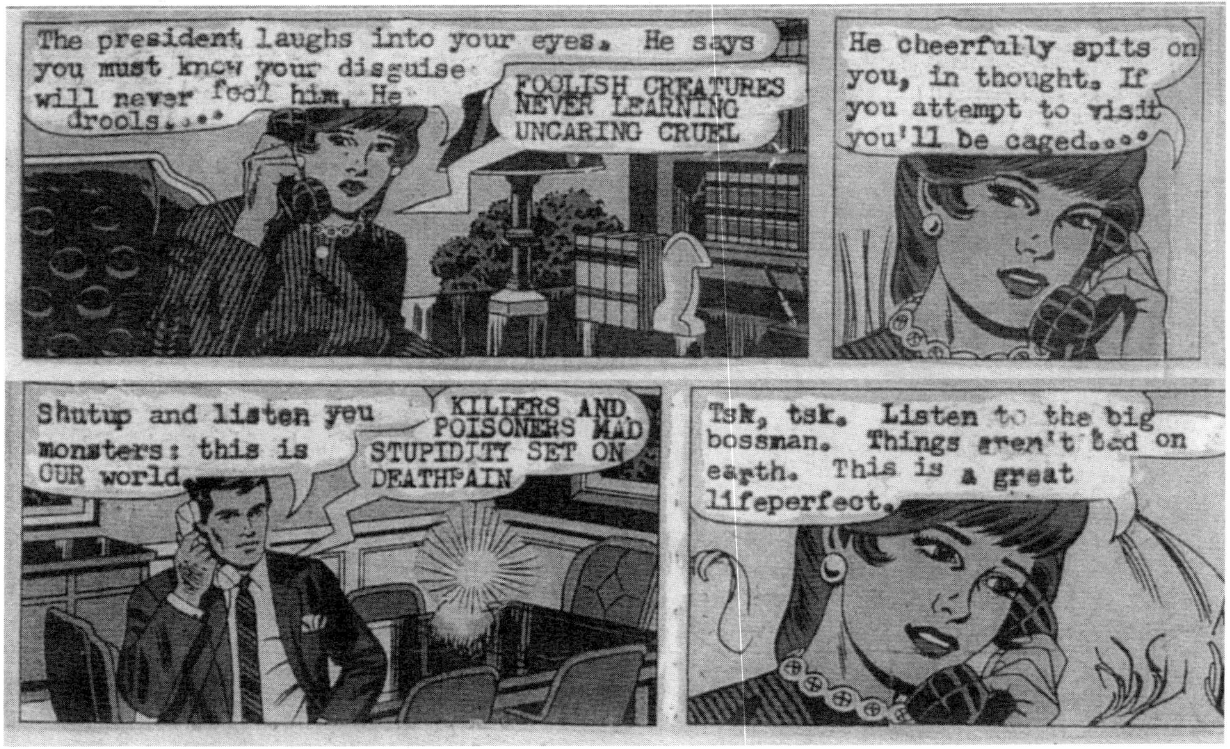
The president laughs into your eyes. He says you must know your disguise will never fool him. He drools...
FOOLISH CREATURES NEVER LEARNING UNCARING CRUEL
He cheerfully spits on you, in thought. If you attempt to visit you'll be caged...
Shutup and listen you monsters: this is OUR world.
KILLERS AND POISONERS MAD STUPIDITY SET ON DEATHPAIN
Tsk, tsk. Listen to the big bossman. Things aren't bad on earth. This is a great lifeperfect.

Ewuare Osayande

Patriotism Imported

and the Betsy Ross you honor
is now a Chinese woman
working 18 hr shifts in Shanghai
wiping the sweat from her face
with the fabric that will become the flag you wave
with pride
but how
when you read the label and find
MADE IN CHINA
why
your patriotism isn't even American made

George Bush II

we have been reeled into
the cinematic debut
of "George Bush Pt. II"
the hole-punched edges of the film
lie beyond the periphery of our lives
and we can't see the name on the director's chair
because of the camera light's glare
and we can't hear our own thoughts
because of the speakers blaring in our ears
telling us to support the president
while he is backstage rehearsing his one line
"we will smoke them out of their caves
and hunt them down"
"we will smoke them out of their caves
and hunt them down"
as he stammers through his lines
his face is being powdered
so we won't see the sweat on his brow
but instead will bow on cue
to his majesty the governor
who stole the crown to become king

acting in the role of a president
playing a 21st century Texas cowboy
cause here
the West is still old and wild
and manifest destiny
means
manifest death.

@ Ground Zero
the criminal plays hero
fiddling while NYC burns
blaming the Muslims
like Nero blamed the Christians
in Rome
@ Ground Zero
we are our people's only heroes
at the bottom's bottom
one with the soil
no stranger to toil or danger
laboring our lives away
born in war-zones
bombed-out homes
from city blocks to cell blocks
our lives are perennially patrolled
@ Ground Zero
where we reside
at the bottom of the rubble
buried beneath charred
steel,
flesh,
stone,
blood,
concrete
and bone
the stench of death floods the nostrils
holding on for dear life
the world's masses

enmeshed in a cacophony of mass confusion
crying out
DOWN HERE!
DOWN HERE!
but no one hears
us
no one hears
yet through all the sorrow
pain and fear
we will remain
there aren't enough of them
to destroy us
all
we
are the world's majority
Viet Nam proved he could no longer win a war on the ground
and after the last bomb has dropped
we will still be here
chanting down your demise
NO MORE LIES!
NO MORE LIES!
NO MORE LIES!
with a record of all the world's dead
with defiance in our fists
and their anger in our eyes.

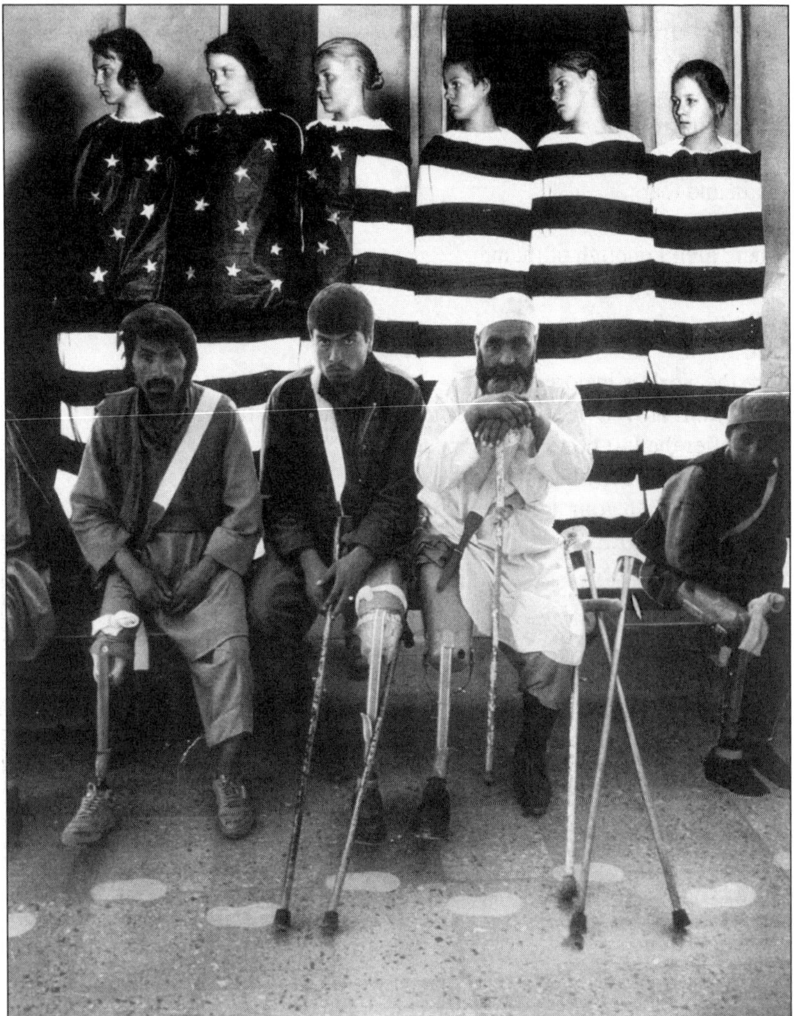

Jen Besemer

Nation

Countries do not feel

the birth of borders
is not from need

you call it loyalty
but nation

is only bridepiece
not duty

your bad bargains
are not my identity

the masters
cannot say my name

Climb

Climb your own heart
weary servant
on the stair of self
your hidden keys sing
your strange teeth

nothing is well now
nothing is right
your silence speaks
in military cadence

grip the wrists
take the flesh
like a prize

stripped to the waist
with arm raised
please

not this

Hogs

Hogs of strife
        creep along the baseboards

and murder trust
        in jaws moist with despair,

they chew their hurt
        and call it honor,

they serve the dynasties
        squatting in the wallow of thought.

Damn those hogs, their acquiescent feet
        sunk again and again

into the mud of lovers and children,
        their tongues licking loss.

They rub the walls of the sty,
        their long teeth reaching

for joy's every apple,
        wanting to own everything they smell.

Kenny Rose

Untitled 1
Fire and sirens,
Exhausted breaths,
Chapped cheeks,
From soaked sleeves.
Green men over oceans
Killing systematically.
Flooding Red Sea
Through mosques and homes,
Staining bed sheets,
Dissolving photographs
With the Final Solution,
Erasing theirstory.

O' thee Holy Property,
The puppeteer is pleased,
Making land a commodity,
A new religion free of spirituality:
A religion of ranks,
Of banks and tanks,
A religion of strings
Pulled by machines.
Men so young and lifeless,
Desensitized by violence,
Distorted dreams of winning
Losing all sense of humanity.

Untitled 2
American media molds Americans into military machines of mass destruction,
Aborting generations to come with white legal lies.
With phallic propaganda preying on prepubescent penises,
They produce hard heads and hands of hate,
To rape for the richest rapists
And with the promise of a raise and an ironic reality show.

Untitled 3

The warm sun on my back,
Something I have not felt
in some time now.
It is just the beginning of Spring.
My skin is burning already.
I do not feel comforted
By the sun and universe.
My expectations are less these days.
How can mothers nuture and comfort
When they are repeatedly raped?
Men so pure and pitiful,
Producers of "progress,"
Fungus of the food chain,
But obliterating other organisms.
They are fathers. they too, give life.
Yet many are just machines,
Molded by myths of masculinity,
Marketing their young men off to offices and cubicles
And off to war to win?
To become men, to live?

Untitled 4

Even the clouds looked violent that day,
And every day since.
The waves wave every which way.
Blood fills the sky and floods the streets.
Across the ocean the deserts have streams now,
For lifeless children to float upon.
Their mothers, and their mothers, and their mothers
Have had seas of salt water for so long before that day.

And these glorious white glows of destruction
Claim to save all civilization from such "barbarians".
If native people of the Old World had known the future,
They might not have differentiated between stars and swastikas.
The farce of the four fathers founding freedom,

Manifested itself into a destiny of an almost infinite edged sword;
Allowing headless horseman to endlessly behead the headed,
Allowing the heartless to deheart the hearted,
With their policies, monopolies, and ideologies filled with hypocrisies,
More murderous than any terrorist attack,
Mass producing more fear and hate for the shelves,
More accesbile than ever before, courtesy of programming,
Programming, programming, programming, programming, programming,
Programming, programming, programming, programming, programming. . .

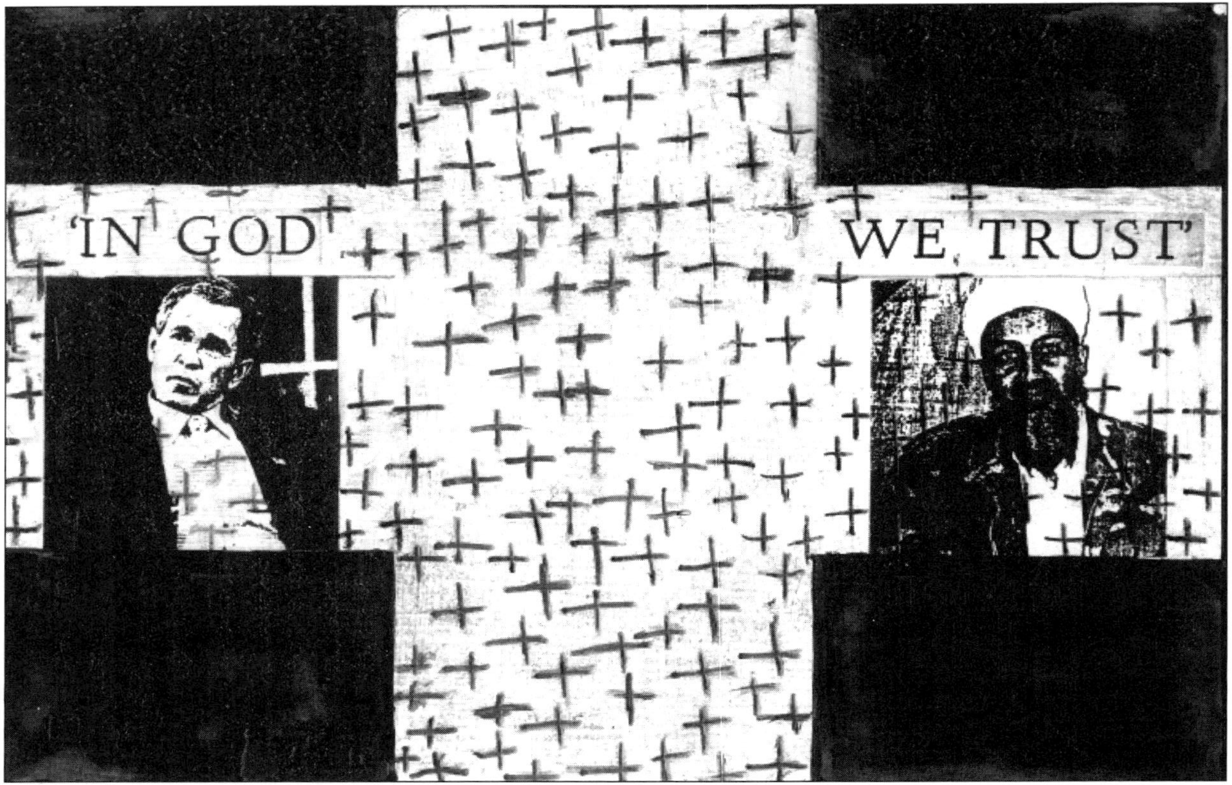
'IN GOD
WE TRUST'

alma khasawnih

thoughts in trumbull-plex (May 3, 2002)

i am not what i seem to be
i am not who you think i am
no ....
you need to start knowing me, dare you talk to me
NO
i am not who you think i am
i am
AM
freedom ...
democracy ...
democracy .... eee whatever the fuck that means
i have a dream
my mother a refugee
i see
her home
Yaffa.
north of tel aviv .... it does not exist anymore
"walk for my return" she said to me
"walk for me" return me
i am a rumbling bubbling volcano
i carry the anger of my people
if you dare look deep in my eyes ... you'll read my rage

throbbing earth quake
intifada
me... i am the wind the tornado
Arab i am. NO... not who you think i am
my blood
a revolution
by birth
by existing
if terrorist is resistance
if terrorist is thought
if terrorist is criticism

if terrorist is anger
if terrorist is brown
poor and fighting
then i am a terrorist.
i am not who you think i am
who i seem to be
i am a volatile arab
i am a revolution
a free revolution
i am resistance
an intifada
when i die
more of me will come
more of me will come

Charlie Burgess

Ergamenes

"The Ethiopian kings of Meroe were worshipped as gods; but whenever the priests chose, they sent a messenger to the king, ordering him to die, and alleging an oracle of the gods as their authority for the command. This command the kings always obeyed down to the reign of Ergamenes, a contemporary of Ptolemy II, King of Egypt. Having received a Greek education which emancipated him from the superstitions o his countrymen, Ergamenes ventured to disregard the command of the priests, and, entering the Golden Temple with a body of soldiers, put the priests to the sword."

—The Golden Bough, Sir James George Frazer

Ergamenes
shopped at Penney's
but he was too large
to open a charge
oh
Ergamenes
where are you now?
we need a fuckin' antichrist
to vacillate the Dow

rite of passage

water boy
ball boy
bat boy

gunman

term limits

Babel, Babel, Babel
that tower's gonna fall
so let's tear it down ourselves
we'll have a fuckin' ball
an' then we'll build another
the tallest in the town
an' have another party
an' tear that fucker down

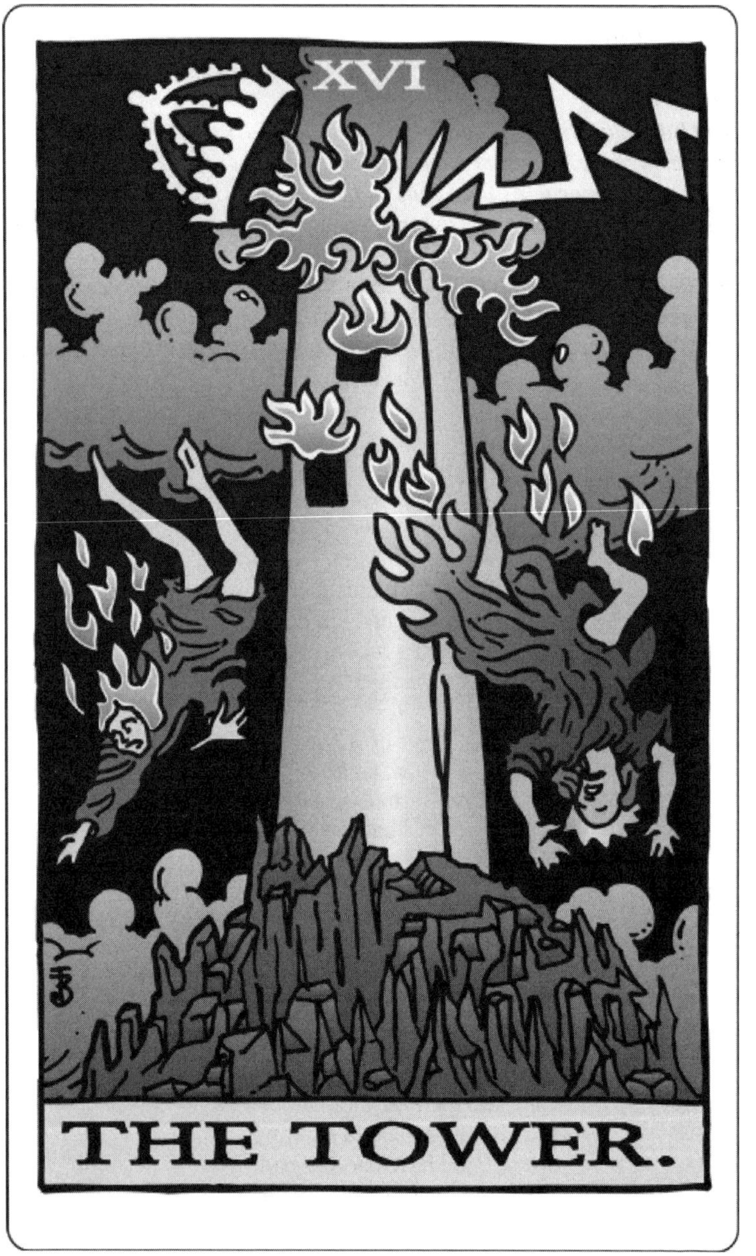
XVI
THE TOWER.

Andy deSantis

the crash
blood
and bodies drip
down the canvas
of the firmament
tears and rage and
amazement
the sheer wonder of
that indian summer
morning — cycles of tears
airplanes and dust
and rubble
every moment into
eternity

into eternity fell
some thousands of lives
men and women
stained business suits
spilt coffee
telephones ring in silence

impalement of machinery
onto bodies like clay
into the cement and
asphalt
surrounding what once were
the tallest buildings in
america

frosted continent
as of 9:48

shaking hands and
broken skin
what once was the strong
hard outer shell of us

naive americans
(or the mainstream of
those thus far)

trees once green and
eager
for this fertile earth
now grey and sullen
and worn
from everything that
once was
to what now is

crystalline

now iced over
bodies and rubble
under the coating
of the long, cold
winter

i am
i am
i am writing this for you
those who were never
recovered from the mess
i am writing for you
the families uncertain
resting uneasy
this is for you
those who will never
be free
which is all of us

death has been our lover
since that crimson
september

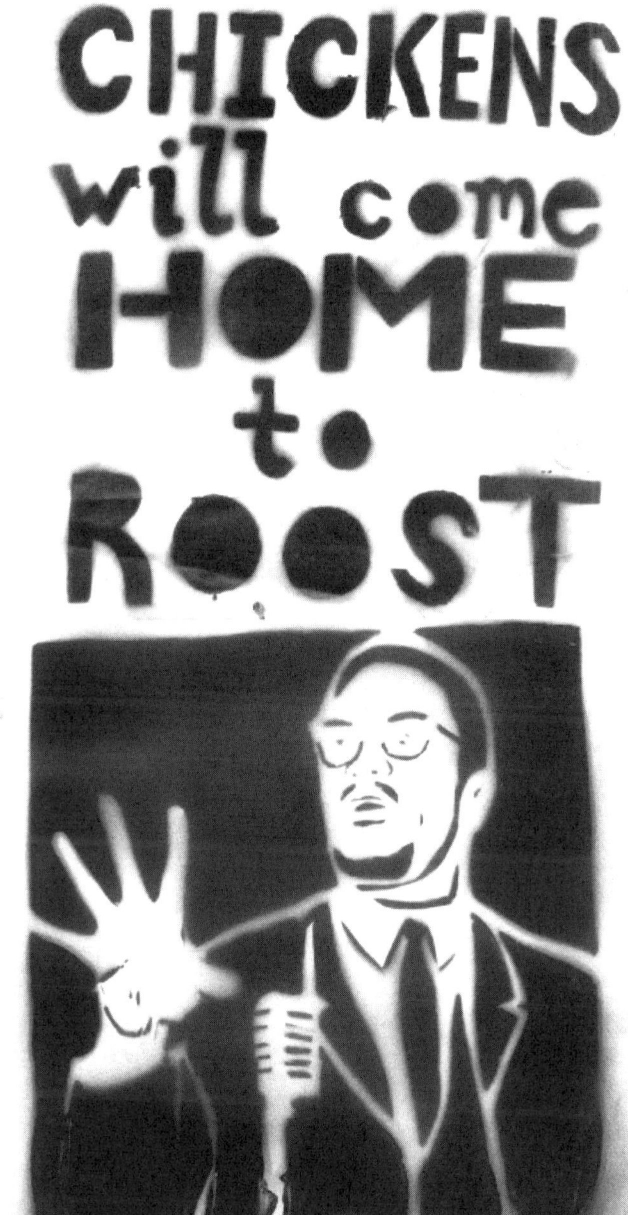
CHICKENS
will come
HOME
to
ROOST

Brian K. Strong

Why do they hate us?
Is it our flag, desire or will?
Maybe it is because of the innocent lives we have killed.

Is it our money or prosperity?
Maybe it is our opposition to other countries right to
Independence and liberty.

Is it our disdain for the inhumane terrorist act?
How can this be when we have used
Terrorist methods to keep unjust foreign
And domestic policies intact.

We used such slogans as "United We stand"
Yet poverty, discrimination and racism run
Rampant and freely throughout the land.

So before you come aboard the ship of patriotism
Ready to raise the flag ask yourself a question
If we are truly on the side of truth and justice
Then please tell me why? Oh, why do they
Despise and hate us?

Susan Bradley

Terror
in the dark eyes of children
and tight grip of refugee parents
on small hands

behind the sidelong glances
engendered by sudden spates
of foreign speech

under a two-minute silence
when carefully unspoken thoughts
detonate bombs

in each shutter-second pronouncement
and every door tightly closed
terror lurks

September 11, 2001
the potential for violence —
for destruction, suicide
or murder lies
in the arsenic in an Appleseed
and in every blade of grass
struggling through concrete

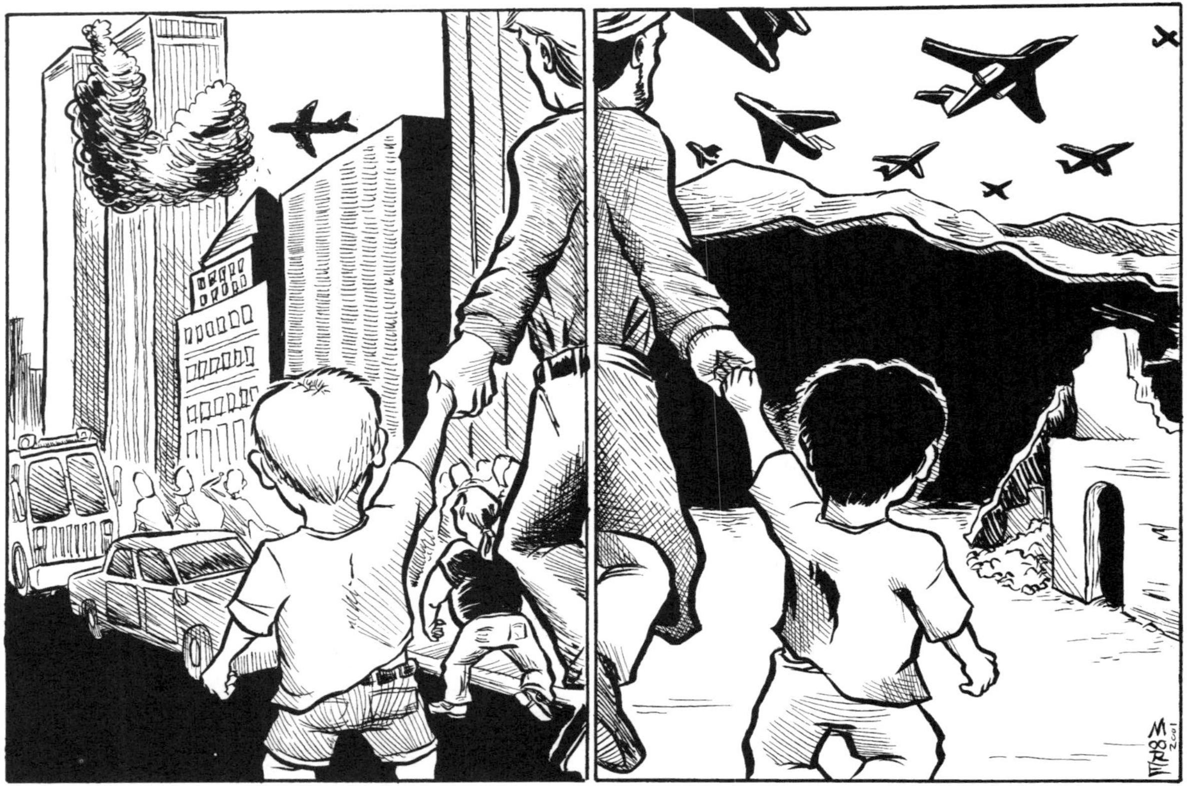

FOR SHAKIR BALOCH (ONE OF THOUSANDS PLUCKED FROM THE STREETS IN THE DAYS AFTER SEPTEMBER 11)

the erupting towers
unleash a fireball
of hatred

rising with the smoke
a cloud of
xenophobic reaction

startling and horrific
as the towers' collapse
it too claims its' innocents

I can hear the shouts
of Shakir Baloch
an unemployed doctor
hopeful in New York
looking for work
as a cabbie
(a familiar injustice)

wrestled to the ground by
New York police,
but they are heroes
aren't they?

under arrest with no reason
suspicious appearance
resembles a terrorist maybe
he has..."that look"

taken to detention
no notice given to anyone
24-hour surveillance
arms bound

solitary

his wife in Canada
frantic for weeks
no word from Shakir

how many more
"disappeared"
(a chilling word we've heard before)

how many more
swept from the streets
after September 11

how many more
still detained
hidden away
arms bound
solitary

without charges
without bail
without trial
without anyone
knowing

Shakir Baloch
is home now
still uncertain why

still wondering
how many more
remain hidden

for this list of victims
is not published
their faces are
far too telling

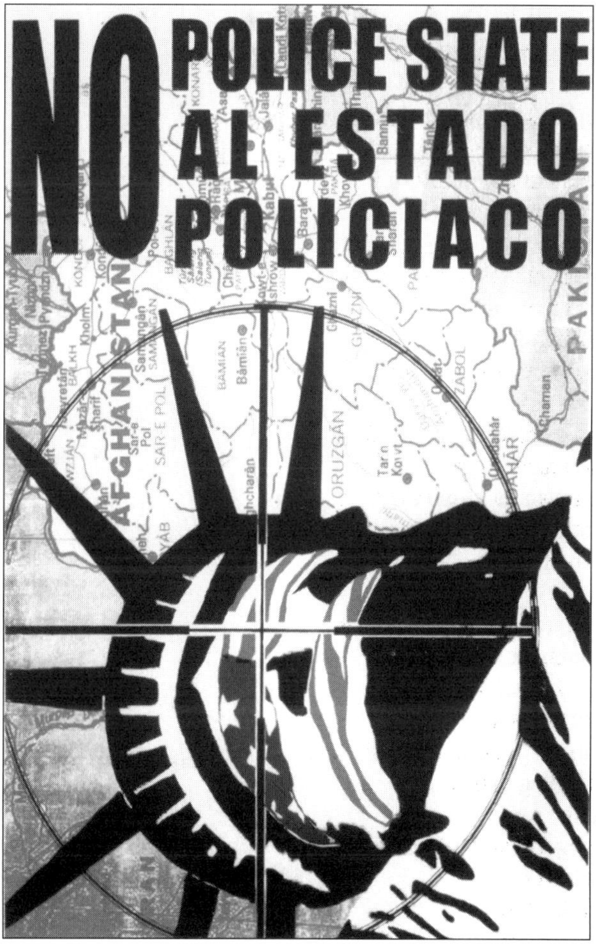
NO
POLICE STATE
AL ESTADO
POLICIACO

D. Blair

The 'What's Colder Than Your Blanket' Statement

so there you sat
cheating yourself
like a fixed game of solitaire
at a broken computer
screening calls from expatriates
quoting quick change predicaments
while the thousand points of light that shine from your eyes
remains interrogative

listening for mistakes and misery
to capitalize upon makes you
the mean man
in anyone's dreams

You don't want to be him, child
You're so much bigger than that
You don't want to climb that tree
To pick at its pockets of rotten fruit
Deadly and frozen

you turn toward heaven and sigh
look through the sky and drag
drag from your cigarette
drag from the race
drag from the back of a pickup truck
it's even a drag to be queen
sometimes
Nicoteenagers can be fickle and fierce
In their clothes
So determined to
Just
Get
Out
  Out of the world

Out of the closet
Out of their minds
This uniform universe is tricking itself
Into treating things badly
Then walking away
From the souls that still need them
As much as the other way round
There's a sharp sound

smack

To catch your attention
To catch you off guard
To catch you
Cold
But what could be colder than your blanket statement

Smallpox and icebergs
Linus on lithium
What?

Who would deny the man with the stone pillow
And the concrete bed
You would America
You offer him one big blanket and until it is wrapped
Tightly around his bony frame
There will be no others

Indeed even when he has killed
Those you told him to kill
He comes home and is still denied

This blanket has strips of fleshy red blood
This blanket got stripes of bone white
Where the meat peeled back
This blanket got a blue field like a
Late night/early morning tv screen

Full of stars

You don't want to climb that tree, Child
The fruit
Will
fall
When it's good
And ready
Fall like thick brown tears
From a scar in the bark
Like a sap
Now's not the time for your tears
Now is the time to move
After the fray and before the feast
Fight hard and love harder

Child,
You don't want to climb that tree,
Simply carve your name in its trunk
To prove you were there and
Move on

Move on to mountaintops
Show some range
Erupt with the love and the kindness I know
You're capable of
It takes strength to be gentle and kind
Courage to be cool and collected
Guts to be reasonable
It takes so much less of these to terrorize and point the finger
Of that, America is King

You don't want to climb that tree, child
You might want to chop that motherfucker down
You may even want to fly an air-fucking-plane

Through its sky

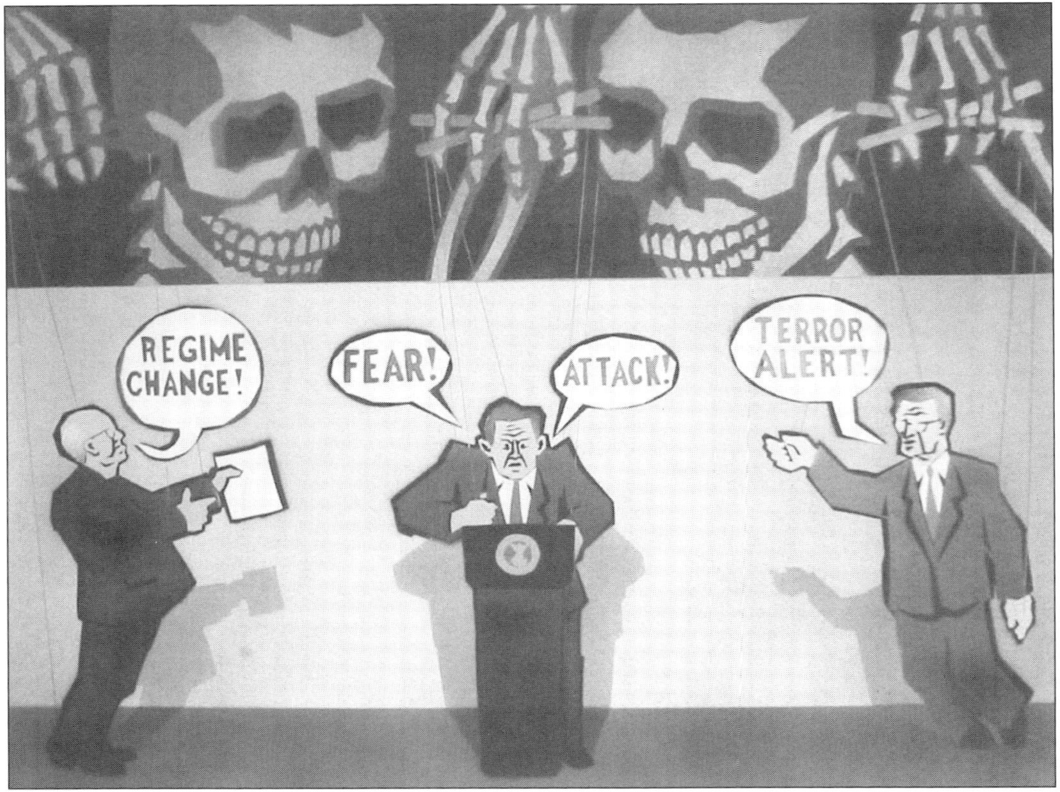
REGIME CHANGE!
FEAR!
ATTACK!
TERROR ALERT!

Sylvia Inwood

Backpedaling to Babylon

Definition of Babylon: 1) a city or place of great luxury, sensuality & often vice & corruption, 2) a place of capitivity or exile.

Did Sacco & Vanzetti die in vain?
75 years later & we are still no closer to liberty
No closer to truth
We are backpedaling to Babylon
With one martyred in Genoa 2001 AS
& half a million children allowed to die in Iraq;
"Not too high a price to pay"
according to Albright,
for America's oil.
& an obscene litany of other lives destroyed all over the planet
& since last September in this land of the free
more than 1,000 held in secrecy without arrest
& without bond for the crime crime of nativity
in the land of Christ's birth

Our fearful leader, himself a burning Bush,
& his corporate masters,
have launched their crusade
in the name of oil,
in the name of greed,
in the name of Mammon
in the name of all that is unholy,
but not in my name!

I will not sacrifice my civil liberties
In the name of Big Brother
With his daily broadcasts of only the news that fits
I will not have my voice silenced for the sake of security
So the masters of war can carry out their plans
Cloaked in the shadows of propaganda

75 years ago, two ordinary working men,
a fish peddler & a cobbler,
my grandfather's heroes,
were railroaded to their deaths by a kangaroo court.
Two ordinary working men were made extraordinary
By circumstances & by their own bravery
Railroaded into death but not obscurity
& not in our name

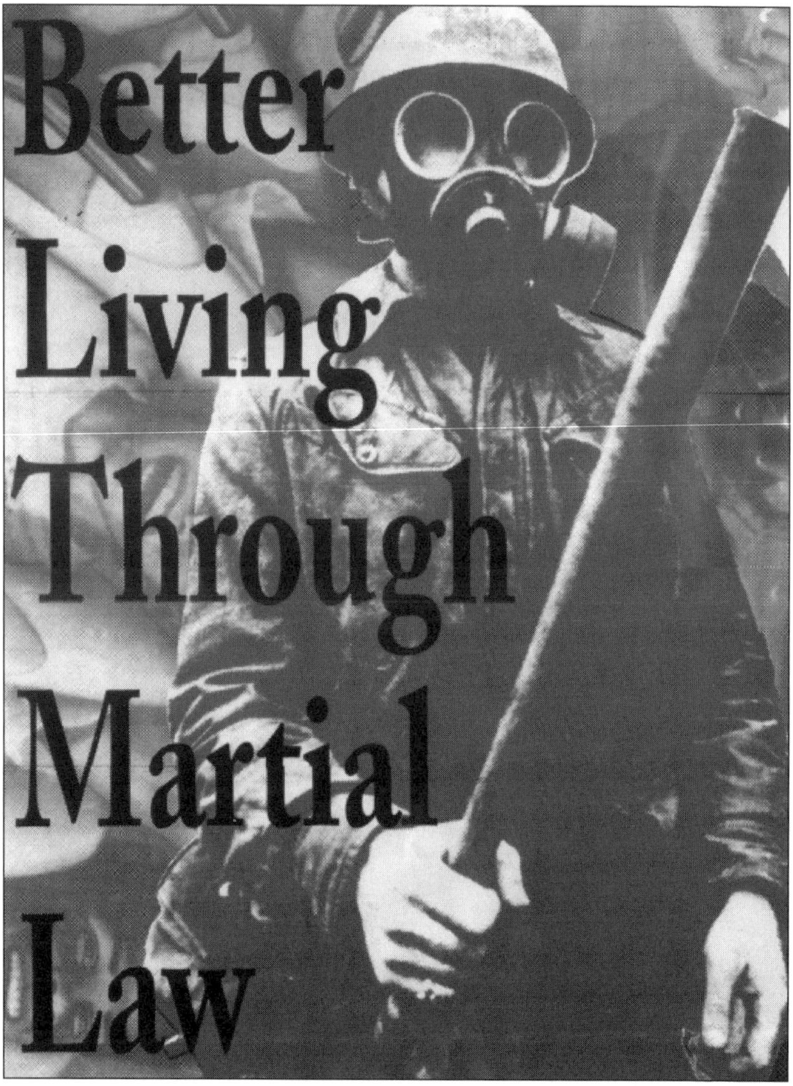
Better
Living
Through
Martial
Law

David Rovics

Hang a flag in the window
We want a safer country
And it's in God we trust
So we'll bomb you during Ramadan
Turn your world into dust
But pull up on your boostraps
And stand on your own two feet
While we blow them off with cluster bombs
Disguised as something to eat

We stand for freedom
And prosperity
So we'll bomb your schools and hospitals
And make sure you live in misery
All you evildoers
And your children and your wives
With our B-52's we'll show you
How we value civilian lives

Give us your hungry, your restless
We'll show you democracy
A military trial
Or detention indefinitely
We'll have homeland security
Thomas Ridge all hail
We may not find the terrorists
But we can throw the left in jail

And we will all be safe
And we shall have no fears
Once our retinas have been scanned
And all the walls have ears
And we're all in good hands
When the FBI is in the know
We're sure they'll look after us

Just like they did with COINTELPRO

(Chorus)
So hang a flag in the window
And all hail to the chief
Follow the leader
And suspend your disbelief
Our country right or wrong
You know what to do
Sing God bless America
Oh that red, white and blue

When facing anyone with boxcutters
We'll say put up your dukes
As we spend fifty billion
On bombers and nukes
We're a beacon of light
And just to make the point
We'll cut taxes on the rich
And throw the poor into the joint
Yes we'll bail out the airlines
Put on your green fedoras
And for all the laid-off workers
We've got maquiladoras
Yes capitalism will save us
For have you ever seen a
More convincing proof
Than Enron and Argentina

(Chorus)

So hang a flag in the window
And all hail to the chief
Follow the leader
And suspend your disbelief
Our country right or wrong
You know what to do

Sing God bless America
Oh that red, white and blue
The Axis of Evil
We'll bomb 'em down the skids
There'll be no more terrorists
Once we kill their kids
People may starve
And economies may crumble
But those folks'll just
Have to learn to be more humble
And give us your money
Debt repayments with aplomb
While we scour the map
For some targets left to bomb
And as another city falls
Upon our sacred American soil
At least we got our Daisy Cutters
And that Alaskan oil

(Chorus)

So hang a flag in the window
And all hail to the chief
Follow the leader
And suspend your disbelief
Our country right or wrong
You know what to do
Sing God bless America
Oh that red, white and blue

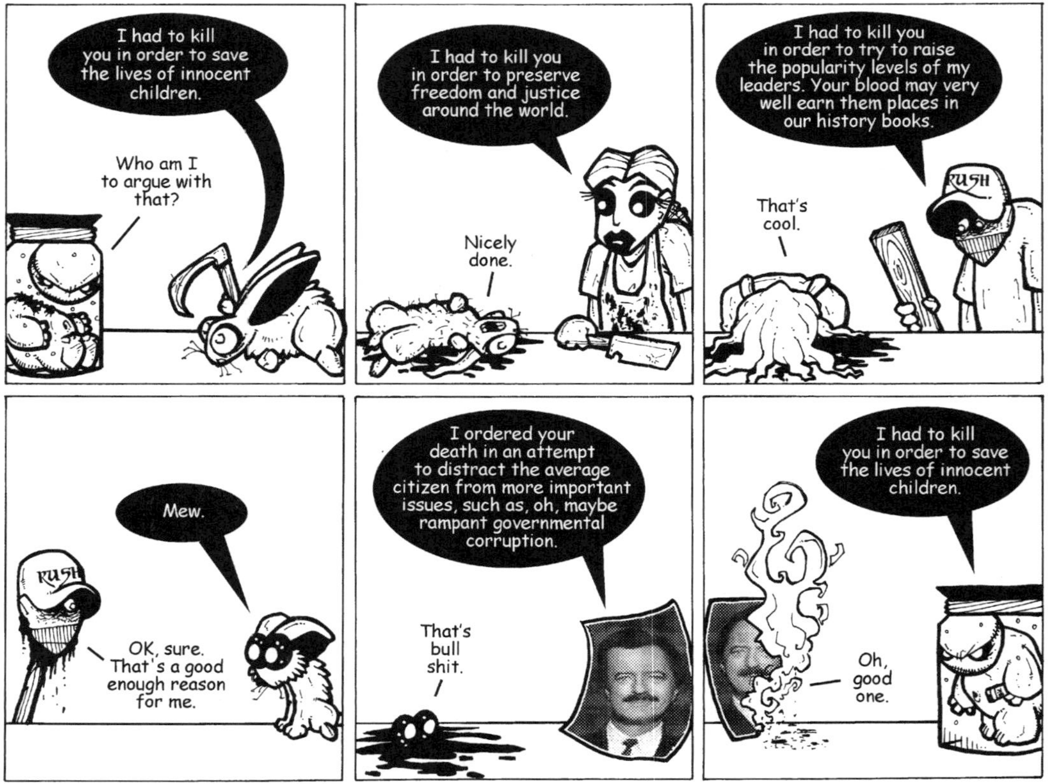

You have a date with Death at: http://www.FetusX.com Sorrow/Millikin 12/21 e-mail: dudes@fetusx.com

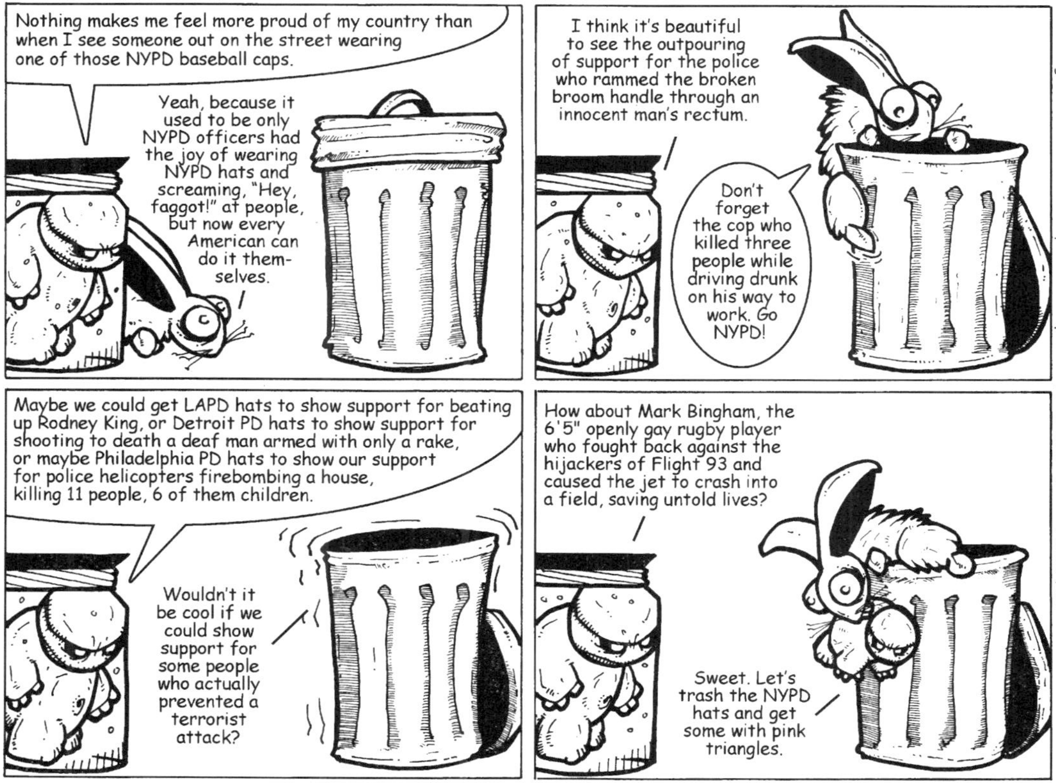

Pink triangles? Aren't those in Lucky Charms: http://www.FetusX.com Sorrow/Millikin 3/1 e-mail: dudes@fetusx.com

Sanjay Bhangar

Kill the Terrorist (formerly known as Love Thy Neighbour)

Over 6,000 people were killed in the State of Gujarat, India. 1,000+ women & girls were raped by mobs of Hindus, often led by leaders belonging to the RSS, VHP and the BJP. In their propaganda leaflets, they often used the Sept. 11th attacks as proof of muslim terrorist ways. By indiscriminately raping women, killing infants, and burning alive whole families, they were only doing their part in the war against terrorism.

I saw blood running down the streets of my country,
I saw women lying by the side of the road,
Raped, murdered.
I saw little children, crying,
Without a home, without a hope.
What has become of my land?
Didn't you know, haven't you heard?
We're all playing this game,
Its called Kill the Terrorist.
Kill, kill, kill the terrorist,
Use gun, use bomb, use fist.
He wears a beard, and he reads a Koran,
Belongs to the enemy, called Pakistan.
Look what he did, look what he's done,
Besides, killing muslims is so much fun.
Kill, kill, kill the terrorist,
Kill father, kill child, be a rapist.
Kill, kill, kill the terrorist,
Didn't you know?
We've just become fascist.
Over 6,000 people were killed in the State of Gujarat.
Some people celebrated this as a victory for the Hindus.
I cried, for my people had won.
What have we done, what have we done?
We have nuclear bombs, we have instant genocide,
Guided missiles in the hands of misguided men.
And for the first time,
I stared into the eyes of the enemy,
Without anything separating us,

No borders, no lies, no propaganda, no hate, no love.
He was suffering the same as I was.
We decided not to kill each other that day.
Kill, kill, kill the terrorist,
My voice is louder than yours.
Kill, kill, kill the terrorist.
Use gun, use bomb, use fist,
Can't you fuckin see? We're fascist.
(ha ha ha ha ha)

Streams of sound-bites, news clips, float through my head…
What is happening to this World…
As people die, as people are murdered,
Someone else is celebrating, someone else is getting richer,
Someone else is getting more powerful, someone's imitating Adolf Hitler.
What have we done, and what have we become?
Enough of this killing,
These armies of hate.
It might not be too late.
Strike out against war,
Strike out against hate.
We need soldiers of peace.
Its time for us to love one another…
Reclaim your spaces, reclaim your heart, reclaim your freedom, reclaim our planet.

Dale Wilson

soldiers' song
blessed is the night
when the bullets are too tired
to come barreling out of their shells
because one day they'll come and I won't be prepared
yeah they'll come and send me right to hell

and the man with the trigger
will try to send me to war
and try to sit me right next to my brother
and if I cross the line i hope he will too
cross the line and walk over the border

so let there be no warrin' for borders
and no warrin' for god
cause if you think fighting is gonna bring back the dead
well im sorry my brother you're wrong

there is a woman shes been waiting for many a month
shes been waiting to hear from a soldier
that she watched from a boy
grow into a man
but from this day he will not grow older

at the station she waits as the minutes tick slow
for her boy that she is so proud of
but the passenger train turns into a box car
its carrying a box that he'll never get out of

so let there be no warrin' for family
and no warrin' for pride
and if you think fighting is gonna bring back the dead
well I guess i can see how you're right

and theres many strong soldiers all across this great land

but not everyone is American
because the one thing we share beyond
color and creed
in the same hole we all can be buried in

so let there be no warrin' for them
and no warrin' for us
and if its a challenge the warrin' hands want
well I say peacfully challenge we must

Mick Vranich

THE TROOPS ARE EVERYWHERE

the troops are everywhere
marching into vacant lots
covered with bones
claiming another border
in the electronic gridwork
the ballistic concerto overhead
whole battalions disappear
in the dust
after the missile attack.
a few miles away
construction crews repair
the highways around the rubble
silhouettes of earth movers
crushing through the haze
to keep the road open
to the internment camps
where the captives
wait for the feed
to be dumped at their feet
walk like the dead
back and forth
empty bags and wrappers
and bottles and cans
scraps of pages from books
tangled in the brush
and barbed wire.
the blue screen glows
day and night
with all the pictures
of what's happening
in the conflicts
highlights and death scores
at the bottom
of the screen.

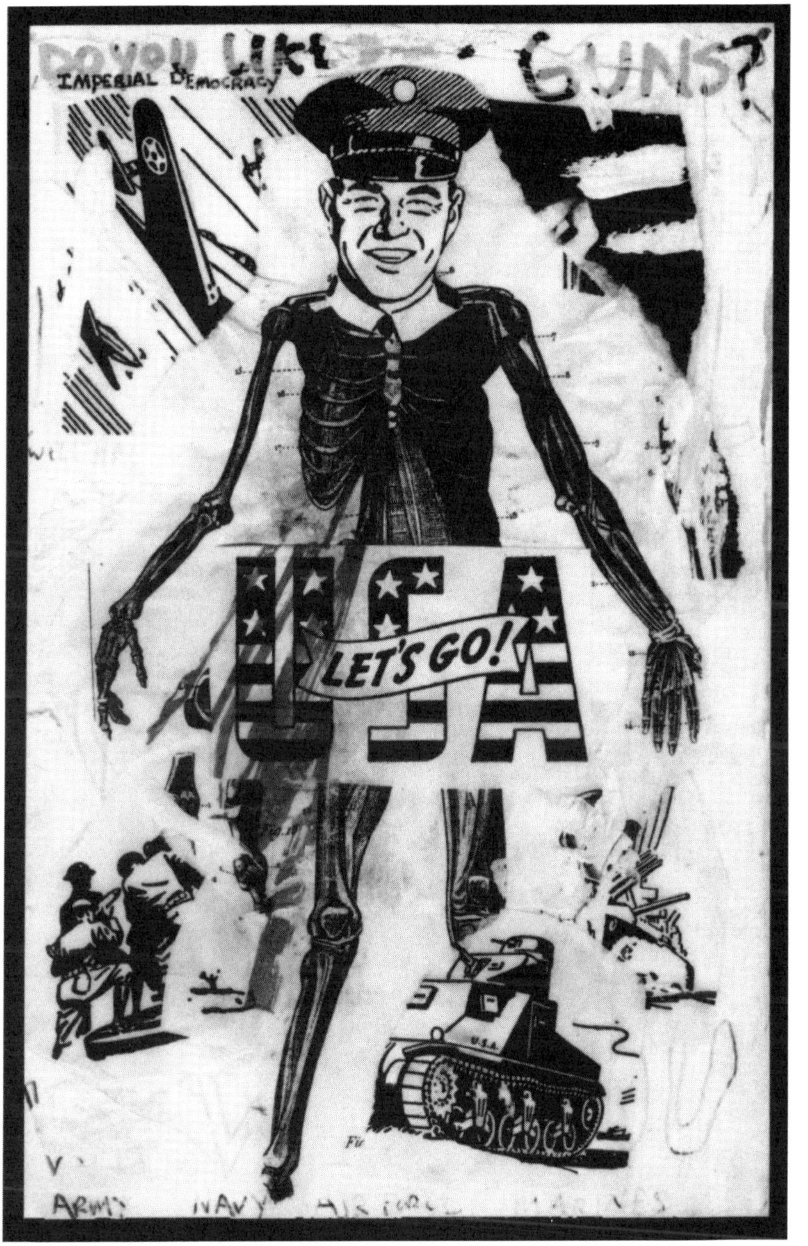
DO YOU LIKE GUNS?
IMPERIAL DEMOCRACY
USA
LET'S GO!
U.S.A.
ARMY NAVY

Patrick J. Kish

White After Labor Day

The human being is an American thing.
It's the all American hamburger king
Under American skies, on American seas,
It's a place where you can be all you can be.
But what could be more? You already free.

To American the beautiful!
And all things holy.
To America the proud!
And the dream is holy.
To America the gleam, and atomic submarine!
To America supreme, super sized, squeaky clean!

It's American, brand new.
It's red, white, and blue.
It's shiny, star-spangled
And goes with my shoes.
I'm so proud and honored I'll bust at the seams.
I can eat like a king.
It's an American thing.

To America the beautiful!
And all things holy.
To America the proud!
And the dream is holy.
To America the gleam, and the atomic submarines!
To American supreme, super sized, squeaky clean!

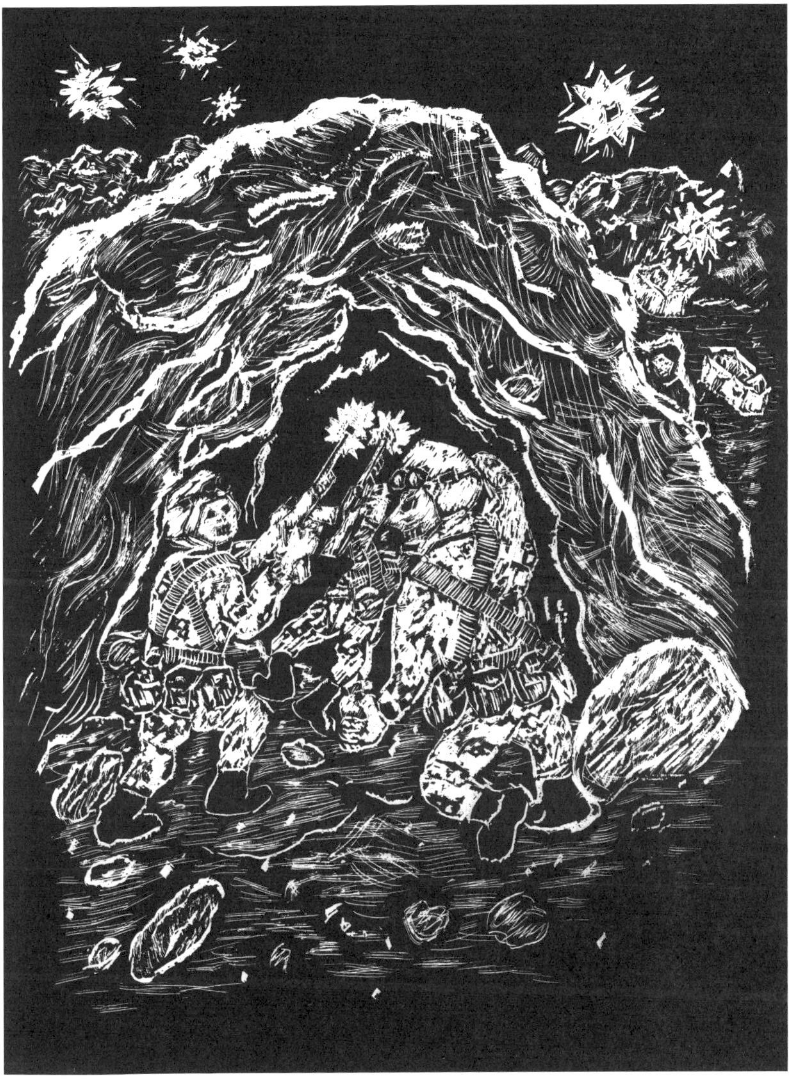

Danté Tucker

Warsong

Honestly, I'd rather watch tv than read, about the worst news,
so for three days straight I'm in the same shorts and shirt too.
Forced to work through what's referred to as a cowardly act to hurt you,
talk sure to reassure you — "It's an attack on American virtue."
They're feeding me the likes of stereotypes worse than watching Urkell,
while our perverse friend the commercial tempts us to be insiders.
They're using quick snippet clips of misinformation to blind us,
while crimes against humanity are rerun to remind us.
They refine some old footage of stoked Muslims to rewind us,
and like a clockwork heart we're set for well timed trust.
While execs work odds behind curtains, like "don't mind us",
we pave a bloody bricked road, leaving lives in the dust.
I wanna believe there's no good reason for legions to fly at us,
but, "do you serve your ego or does it serve you?" — cause mind does.
So I'm only proportionally proud of the past that we have behind us,
shouting to a mountain of accountants where the cable line's from-
You should wise up! Don't revise the causes of why they despise us,
using lies to fill up children, shielding them instead of buildings.
While a pair of them burn, you watch with stares of concern,
Preach that hate on American dirt, create the same heritage of hurt.
This is warfare that's not fair, it's war through the media
controlled by those trying to close our only means to compete with them.
It's war from these "authorities" born to be leaching us,
yet it's all funded by millions of dollars that come from each of us.
And we believe this stuff, the working class people of America,
both the most ignorant and most important of all the characters
in secret wars for territories kept from us like a parent does
the true stuff too brutal for the youth to bear at all.

Obedient drone bees when they appeal to our egos,
we start piping stars and stripes like everywhere we go.
Barking with their hype is all we know,
and that's the thanks that we give them.
Swoll heads are falling victim to the anthem of patriotism.

Brandon Bauer

History 101.

No,
I'm not surprised—

I'm not surprised that the terrorists killed...the opposition killed... the peacekeepers killed...the freedom fighters killed...the religious zealots killed...the paramilitaries killed...the fundamentalists killed...the rebels killed...the colonial powers killed...the insurgents killed...the special forces killed...the communists killed...the fascists killed...the strike breakers killed...the nationalists killed...the puppet dictators killed...the corporate private army killed...the lone wolf killed...the federal agent killed...the mercenaries killed...the patriots killed...the clandestine operatives killed... the partisans killed...the police killed...the fanatics killed...the imperialist powers killed...the indigenous people of the world...

Power kills, greed kills—fanning the flames:
Nationalism, Ideology, Ethnicity— the quest for wealth.
The history of ours is a heist story,
Stolen lands... broken promises

Enslaved people.
Nameless souls buried in mass graves.
—civilization

—Genocide

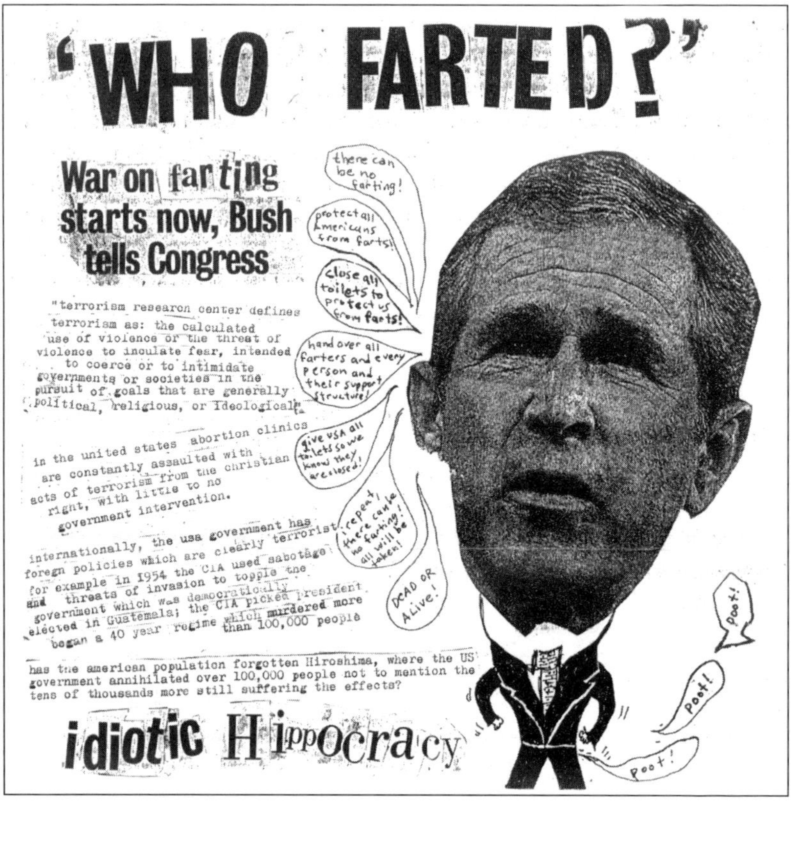
'WHO FARTED?'
War on farting starts now, Bush tells Congress
"terrorism research center defines terrorism as: the calculated use of violence or the threat of violence to inculate fear, intended to coerce or to intimidate governments or societies in the pursuit of goals that are generally political, religious, or ideological"
in the united states abortion clinics are constantly assaulted with acts of terrorism from the christian right, with little to no government intervention.
internationally, the usa government has foregn policies which are clearly terrorist for example in 1954 the CIA used sabotage and threats of invasion to topple the government which was democratically elected in Guatemala; the CIA picked president began a 40 year regime which murdered more than 100,000 people
has the american population forgotten Hiroshima, where the US government annihilated over 100,000 people not to mention the tens of thousands more still suffering the effects?
idiotic Hippocracy
there can be no farting!
protect all Americans from farts!
close all toilets to protect us from farts!
hand over all farters and every person and their support structure!
give USA all toilets so we know they are closed!
i repeat, there can be no farting! all will be taken!
DEAD OR ALIVE!
Poot!
Poot!
Poot!

the hipcriticals
(an all girl acapella generic hiphop outfit from pittsburgh, pa)

terrorist attack
terrorist attack
america strikes back
with a war plan
bombs shower down over the taliban
and the patriots, the prey to god
while islamic militants are on a jihad.

the towers tumble
america crumbles
gettin' weak at the knees
time to heighten homeland security...

well the resistance movement has been growing
BOOM BOOM BOOM
did america start this war to stop the impending doom
It's the end of state power
the final hour
for capitalism
uh oh! upsurge of nationalism
a jingo jango raise that flag
you put'em on your cars you put 'em on your trucks
if your shop don't have one
YOUR BUSINESS IS FUCKED
funny how the flagwavers can't even share the road
when i'm riding my bike, they squash me like a toad

after all the bombs and nuclear submarines —
the beds of the dead will still be cold
(we said the beds of the dead will still be cold,
as the war grows old)

northern alliance allied with u.s. troops
and glory old england lacing up their combat boots

and the pakistani government is lending their land
to UNCLE - MOTHER- FUCKING- SAM
and the pakistani people riot and demand
screaming NO LAND for UNCLE SAM
they're yelling NO LAND for UNCLE SAM
they're dying for their land

osama and bush in their ivory towers
money lets 'em cower
while the poor - old - schmucks-
are - on -their - way
their gonna
their gonna
their gonna
their gonna DIE GONNA DIE GONNA DIE FOR THEIR
GOVERNMENT DIE FOR THEIR COUNTRY
THAT'S SHIT......BOOM ANOTHER BOMB JUST HIT*

yo the people in afghanistan eat locusts for protein
you know what i mean...they ain't got shit...BOOM
ANOTHER BOMB JUST HIT

(then we do hand clap games like kids do
and in a slow sing songy way end with this)

the world trade centers all still all gone
and the u.s. has dropped the bomb
hey george bush, not so fast have you taken a look,
a look at our past
guatemala.............mexico
nicaragua..............and puerto rico
the phillipines.......kosovo
colombia...............iraq
just a few examples of america striking back

**this is a sample from an anti-flag song*
anti-flag also hails from pittsburgh

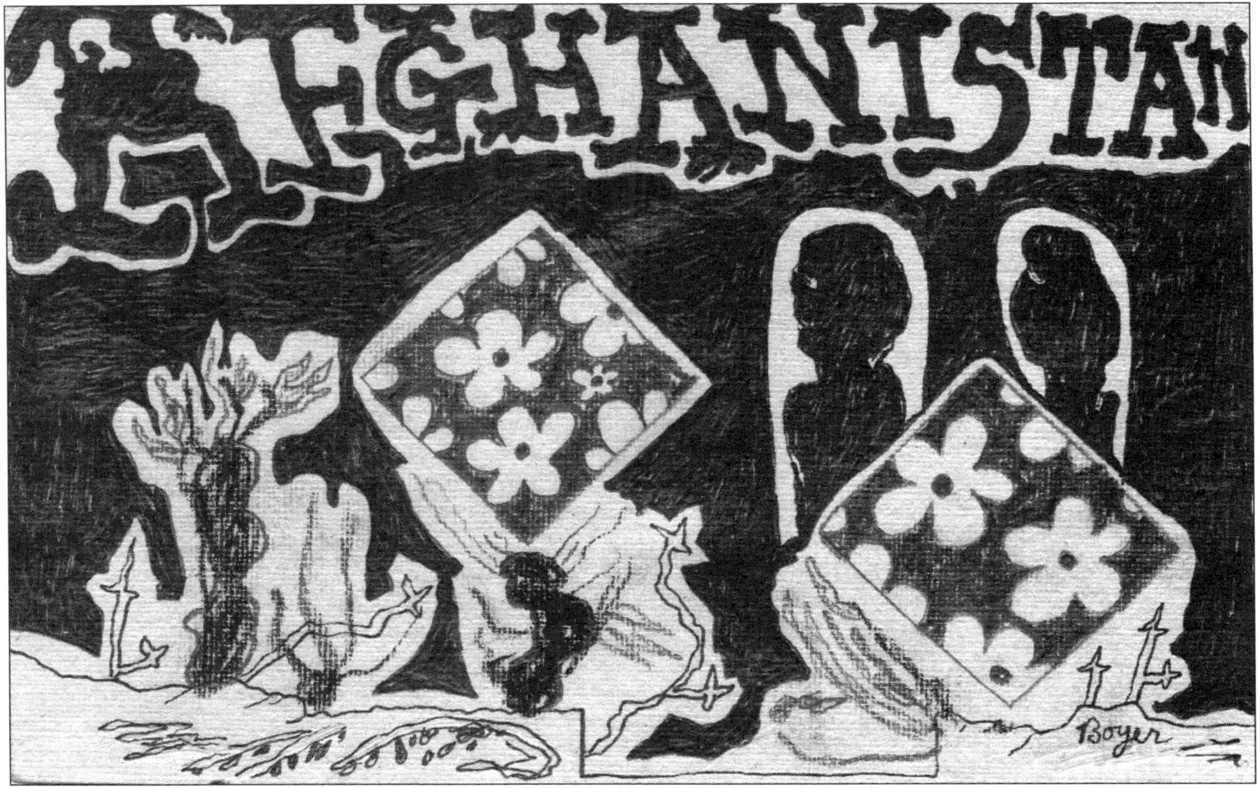
AFGHANISTAN
Boyer

Scott Farrow

The last laugh
your pristine altar is stained with blood;
father, please tell me why this is so
will your sacrifices turn back the flood,
or change the way the wind blows?

the weapon in your hand is stained with blood;
brother, please tell me why this is so
will your triumph bring an end to war,
or only add to the number of foes?

time will tell what will be,
the years will solve the mystery
your deeds write your epitaph-
time will have the last laugh

your golden throne reeks of intrigue;
the murderer's blade,death's final plea
does your power justify the means,
or the ends of your extremes?

your wealth,your gold,ring like the steel;
you used in murder to close the deal
do your ghosts wake you up at night?
do you wait for death at dawn's light?

will your crimes serve to set you free?
will your tears dissolve the misery?
your deeds write your epitaph-
your history's final paragraph-
time will have the last laugh

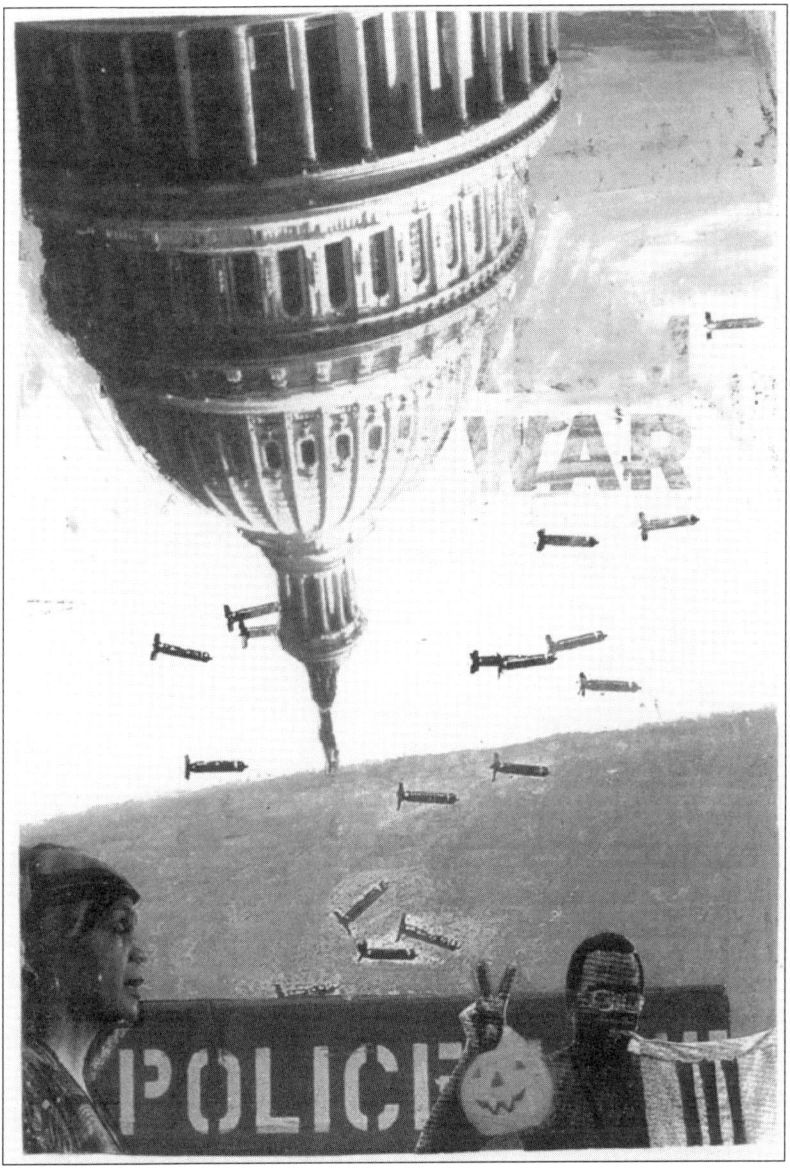
WAR
POLICE

Revelation!

ya know that BIG HOUSE

on that downsouth plantation

that got vanquished in the Civil War?

well now,that BIG HOUSE

is the WHITE HOUSE

and that plantation

is the WHOLE WORLD!

As Dream, As Movie

did you see it?
did you see it?
you saw it.
you saw it.
i saw it.
they saw it.
we saw it.
it was the MOVE bombing
times three thousand.
times three thousand.
it was WACO only bigger.
it was Tulsa, Oklahoma only bigger
did you see it?
you saw it.

it was reality as dream,as movie
as the real real
it was unbelievable!
believe it. believe it.
there's more!
there's more!
there's more!
are you ready?
there's more!
are you ready?
are you ready?

Fate

when we speak the TRUTH
they call it HATE

when their empire is in ashes
we'll call it FATE

Morgan Guyton

Winter Begins
It does no good to scream
with one wet syllable
winter can white out your words.

"Move! Move!"
The ghost baton
finds all the skin
that it needs.

"War's not worth the weight of sleet,"
shrug the trees,
"Just drop your leaves and go."

The wind will not negotiate;
it speaks through a bullhorn.
"Don't stop; don't look at me;
Do you want your eyes to bleed?"

The snarls of ice-dogs
slice through thickets
off squatting families.

The panic bells are drawn
and bugles begin
to carpet the landscape.

A million trembling hands
fiddle with new uniforms
the march begins-

Snow too thick for horizons,
steps too quick to leave footprints,
hands concealed,
eyes only on the boots ahead.

If only the snowprints held their history...
If only we had a compass...
"We need a fire!" somebody shouts.

You gather up the forest's bones
into an altar;
from spittle and sneers,
the arms of a cedar
shield the young kindling.

Yes, *you blow*
through cracks too small for no,
and soon a new mother
has laid her first coals.

In time, the young furnace
gains a voice.
Other fire-starters
signal through the fog.

A crowd has gathered-
watching till we're warm enough to sing;
singing till we're soft enough to cry.

As courage opens up our lungs,
we shout over the blizzard;
more people stop.

Winter screams even louder,
lashing the legs of the curious:
"Move along! Just move along now!"

But now our forest blaze
has stopped the flow of traffic,
our bodies form a barricade,
for which winter reads us our consequences.

We will get sprayed
till the frost holds open our eyes;
our lips will seal shut;
we may lose fingers.

But if we all stand close enough
and cover the hope with our hands,
if our smiles become mirrors
and our eyes become torches,
if we wipe each other's cheeks
and tie our sweaters together,

Then we can refuse to march this winter.

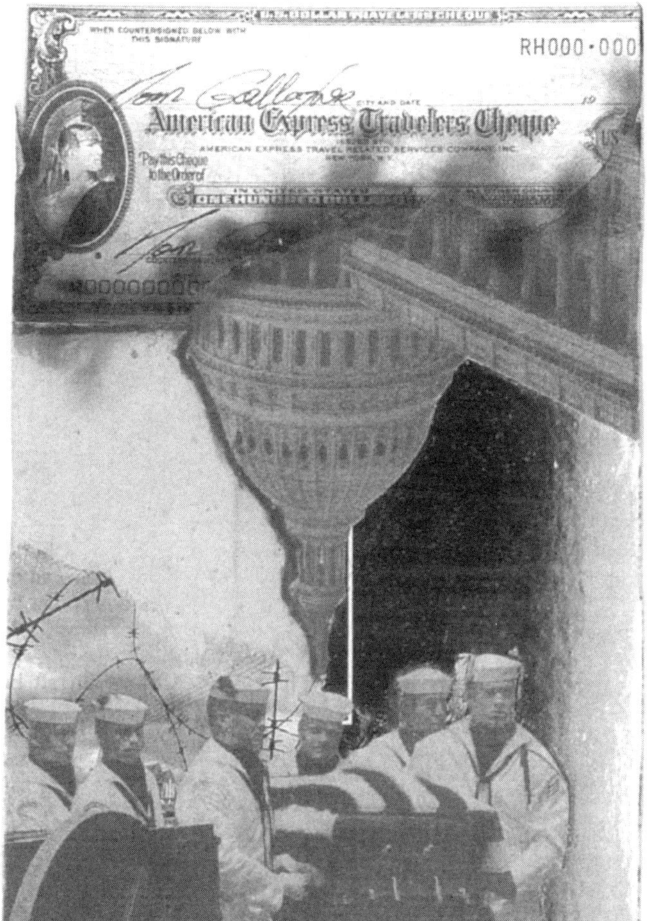
WHEN COUNTERSIGNED BELOW WITH
THIS SIGNATURE
RH000·000
American Express Travelers Cheque
AMERICAN EXPRESS TRAVEL RELATED SERVICES COMPANY, INC.
Pay this Cheque
to the Order of

Mary Ann Cameron

Spirit 9 – 11
The only thing that dark
needs to advance is
for light to recede

to find itself sucked back into
our pettinesses our greeds
our moments of lies and
secrets our crimes our
rationales

personal local national
our misunderstandings
about religion alone

our fears

the only thing that edges
back the dark is for our
light to shine on it

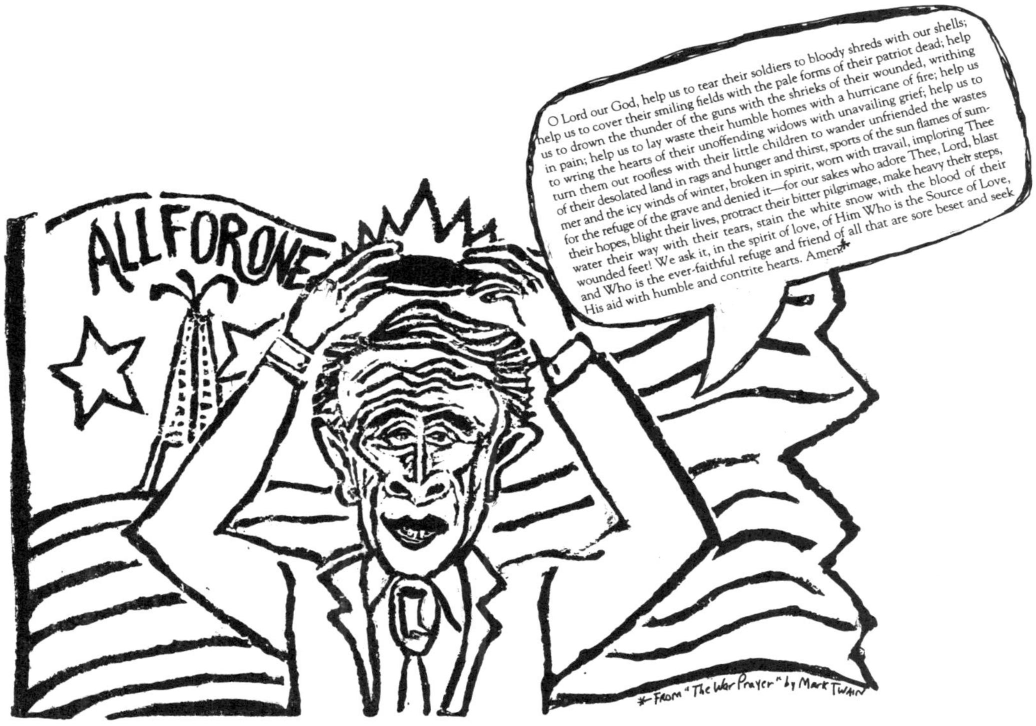
ALL FOR ONE
O Lord our God, help us to tear their soldiers to bloody shreds with our shells; help us to cover their smiling fields with the pale forms of their patriot dead; help us to drown the thunder of the guns with the shrieks of their wounded, writhing in pain; help us to lay waste their humble homes with a hurricane of fire; help us to wring the hearts of their unoffending widows with unavailing grief; help us to turn them out roofless with their little children to wander unfriended the wastes of their desolated land in rags and hunger and thirst, sports of the sun flames of summer and the icy winds of winter, broken in spirit, worn with travail, imploring Thee for the refuge of the grave and denied it—for our sakes who adore Thee, Lord, blast their hopes, blight their lives, protract their bitter pilgrimage, make heavy their steps, water their way with their tears, stain the white snow with the blood of their wounded feet! We ask it, in the spirit of love, of Him Who is the Source of Love, and Who is the ever-faithful refuge and friend of all that are sore beset and seek His aid with humble and contrite hearts. Amen*
* FROM "The War Prayer" by Mark Twain

David Sands

all the days after

all the days after
in the television universe
the footage wouldn't stop crashing
the planes crashes
the towers crashes
the fires crashes crackles crashes
the flags and speeches and wars crashes
and crashes

in the television universe
the wreckage inside us
never crashes

our empty jobs
never crashes
our rotting city
our lack of love
our violation
our pained silence
our self destruction
our hands on the steering wheel
never crashes
in the television universe

but inside us
all around us
they crashes
everyday
for all our lives
they crashes

crashing
until we stop crashing
until we get out of the wreckage

until we stop sitting in the rubble
crashing
until we stop crashing

and start to build
our lives
ourselves
today
and all the days after

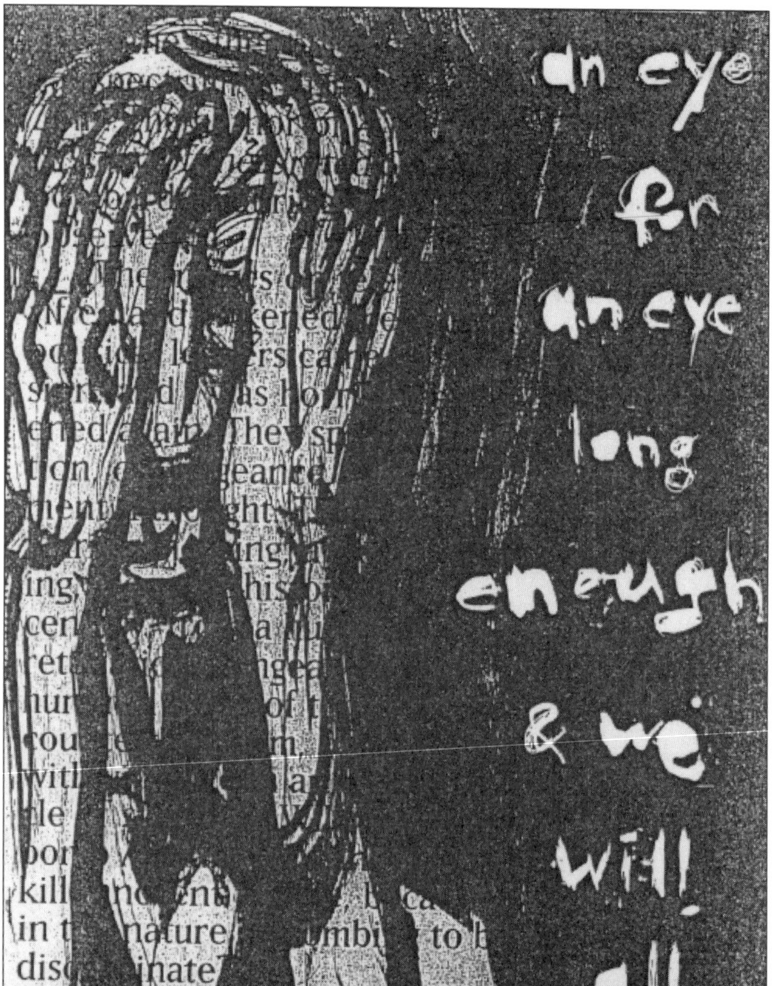
an eye
for
an eye
long
enough
& we
will
all
go
blind

Jhon Clark

Sleep is a storm
[part 1]
Prone to toss and turn   Left and right   Over and
over
At the center   Is a force that struggles—to get a
hold of this
Sleep is a storm
Inside a cyclotron   Whisper Power and   Wake!
Walking then running   tripping   falling   healing
Do nothing to do something
Listen and organize   Treadmill fast
The Freedom Movement phrases burrow in seeking shelter

And like the moon effects the sea   all these words
they effect me
they give me hope
even though
Dignity is quiet (it's not all busted or broke)
Direct action is worried so resistance is   stable and
secure   only
The night is still bright with opportunity
Daydreaming they're phases   Not phases
No Not phases   Phases can't last
Thinking   thinking   Over and over   each to
their ability
each to their ability
Participate in the expression
Will will will
Power- ill   haven
I
or won't I
Sleep

[day2]
Wake
Walking toward caffeine hitting my head
Falling it shakes loose and uncovers
HIS-story
Slave Codes were rewritten as the Black Codes
Slave Codes were rewritten as the Black Codes
Slave Codes were rewritten as the Black
Codes
Said three times like
Three Strikes
write write write
Fall fall fall into
Realization Reinterpretation Regurgitation and
Elucidation

Racism Racism Racism

Sleep wake sleep wake organize resist struggle too
much at stake
Sleep wake sleep wake organize resist struggle do I
need a break?
Hit the snooze
I'm awake already
I'm awake I'm awake I'm awake
Lean back lean on drivc away visit family
God damn got to relax no got to move
fast no
Crash and crash
And crash

Read

Won't phrases become beliefs Paragraphs words
Sounds poems Life poetry
On my own terms and in my own words

[part 2]
Uncover histories
So devastating   this slaughter
Cry cry cry   dream a blurred vision
Roar with anger
Dream of Roman ancestors and their children
Descending from ignorance
Ascending to knowledge
The tree she took from was poisoned by The Man
And the idea of a man as god

The theory informs practice
The vision informs strategy
The theory informs practice
I said
The vision informs strategy

Sleep well   sleep well   organize   relax
sleep well little friend
But for 90%   90% of the victims of
war are civilians
the children are being sacrificed
And 94% of HIV infected   live in poor countries
94%
13 million people hungry everyday
$1000 a plate
Party fundraisers
They say You pay
We pay   Yea we pay   as a matter of fact like there's
no tomorrow or today
Sleep is a storm

Days are Rage
Property. Destruction.
Deep Discussion Art and Agitation
Change this System
Revolution revolution   a bloody fucking revolution

does what!

Tired people
Tired people like me can see
Yes
We need revolution to be free
I can see
Education collectives Community institutions Less excuses
Now
Not private corporations or a State
Awake awake
Screaming of love
Because they hate

Learning the people's stories
Potosi
Magellan...nothing but a slaver
They clear mountains and mine
Decimate tribes
The Ohio Company The Charleston Port The Gold Coast
The history of greed named
It spells out The United States

[part 3]
Here are the addresses of their descendants
maybe stop by
maybe say hi and ask them
Why are you so wealthy
You are a thief and a murderer protected
An international thief leaving a trail of dead

Maybe they do need a bullet in the head
Maybe

This "world system" defended Power and Privilege

Protected
So goods are traded
It's never truly benefited   All
In truth the poor are paying for it

We want peace   better farming and   more wood carving
Cooking and caring
Even astronomy and knitting
Not
Men dominating   offering depression
Expectin' their power served to 'em
Never!
Never!

[All the Days After]
I'm sleeping better now and not so in a hurry
Look into my eyes
They're not dulled from substances
Or brand names or even my fury
I have integrity and humility   won't you join me
I can laugh aloud   jump up and down
Knees rising
Left fist pumping
Feet landing   rhythmically

In the street   Door to door
We want more
In the street   Door to door
We want more

Fuck. Your. Racist. War(s)

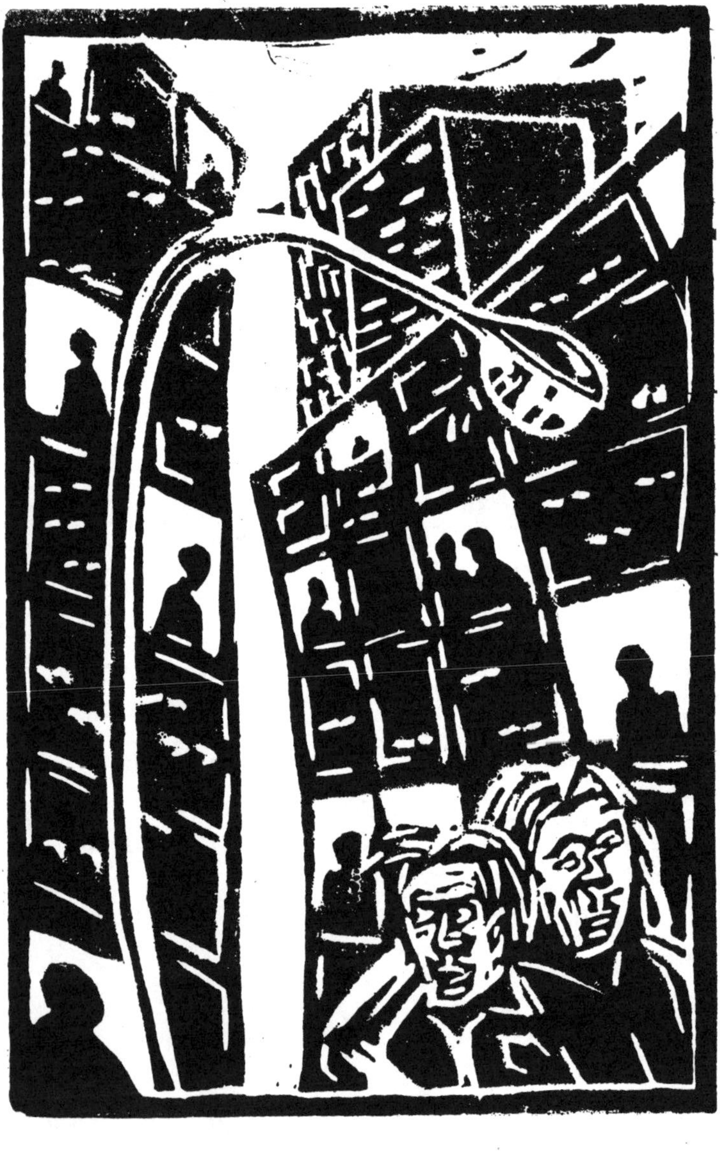

B. Kirwin

Evolution

Today I left the city
The skeletons trapped in the drywall
Scratching regrets
Into the chipping paint

My feet dance
Their voodoo way
Along rays of light
Stretched long and grotesque
Centuries spent
On a medieval torture rack

I shrink as I go
Until I am no better
Than a blade of grass

This is where I come to the edge edge of the wood
And the warped light
Of the dying sun
Is replaced by a glow
Like effervescent moss
I am caught by it
And pulled into it
I try to speak
But only swallow silent answers

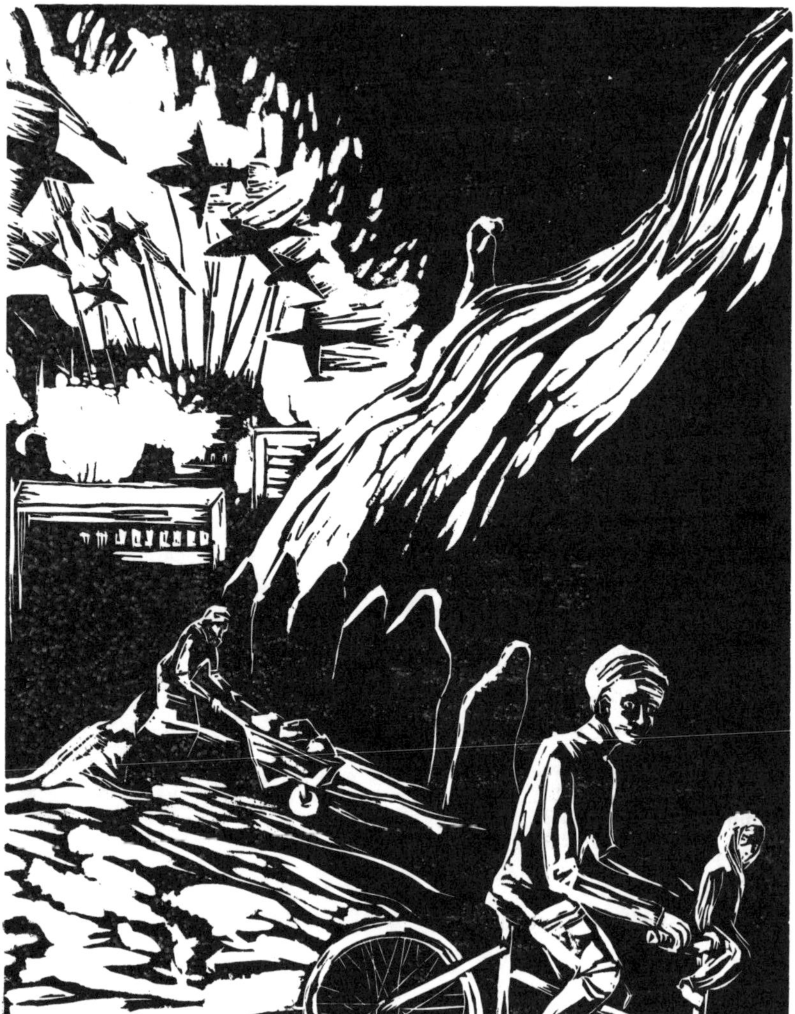

The British daily Guardian correspondent, Ian Traynor, reported that the following scene in Charakar, Afghanistan was a normal one: "A three-year-old girl was perched on the handlebars of a bike being pedalled north by her 14-year-old brother, and an old man pushed a wheelbarrow as fast as he could up the road away from the war ...
women in flight were a ghost-like night, shuffling in the pitch dark, cloaked in their all-covering burqas, carrying babies in their arms and ragged bundles on their heads."

8 October 2001

Shailja Patel

Eater Of Death

Based on a report from http://www.rawa.org of a woman whose husband and seven children were killed at breakfast by US air strikes on Kabul

<u>One</u>

They came as we ate breakfast, I remember the taste
of black market naan.
Zainab and Shahnaz turned eyes like whirlpools
as I sprinkled them
with precious water.
My children ate slowly,
slowly,
tasting each crumb.
I remember the bitterness in my throat.
Before we finished
the sky ripped open, vomited
death, everything
fell around us, everything
burned, children screamed, walls shattered
a voice like a jackal's howled

Kamal Gohar Shahnaz Sadiyah Zainab Zarafshan
On and on, after all
the other noises
stopped

Kamal Gohar Shahnaz Sadiyah Zainab Zarafshan
split my head, I would have beaten it
into silence.
I raised my hands
to block my ears, my fingers fell
into the well
of a hole in my face
the howling

came from me.

Two

Three days later,
in the shelter,
thick with the stench
of human waste, of terror,
starvation and nausea
fought like mujaheddin
in my gut.
Aziza, my neighbour,
shards of rubble
still in her matted hair,
showed me
a package. Yellow
like the bombs. With an
American flag.
She said:
They say it's food.
Tears gouged tracks
in the dirt on her face,
her mouth twitched, her head jerked
her one remaining hand shook, spittle and words
jumped from her lips:
Food coloured like
the bombs. For the children
still alive
to pick from minefields
with the hands
they still have left.

And finally I understood

the savagery of a people
who would gloat
over those they kill,

who would take the limbs,
eyes, sanity
of their victims
before execution. I cried out
to the shelter roof, dark as a coffin:
Have they no mothers
no children
in America?

Three
On the ninth day,
after Aziza died
still clutching the pack
she refused to open,
I pried it from her lifeless
lacerated fingers, I
ate the food.
The blood and bones and fat
of my children,
in a yellow pack,
with an American flag.
I ate the names
I'd patted into my belly
as they ripened inside me,
one by one. The names
that angered
their father,
who said, in his despair:
What future have they
in this country that's meat
for wolves?
I answered him:
Each of them
is a miracle of life, I will not
dim their wonder.

Kamal – perfection, how you bruise
and scrape my abscessed tongue.
Gohar – diamond, precious stone,
now break my loosened teeth.
Shahnaz – princess, red gelatinous heart
of this monstrous American pastry,
I smear you on my mouth.
Sadiyah – blessed one, sink in my stomach,
stone of my womb, I take you back.
Zainab – granddaughter of the Prophet, peace
be unto him and you, sugar
my saliva, prophesy
what comes to eaters of death.
Zarafshan –
Zar- af – shan, littlest one, I named you
for a mighty river. You taste now
of rancid mud, you taste now
of poisoned fish,
littlest one
you taste
of splintered glass.

Four

Their names will not be remembered,
they are not American.
Museums will not hold their relics, they are not
American. No other mother's
children will be murdered
in their memory, they are NOT
American.
But I?
I have eaten
from the bowels of hell,
chewed and swallowed
the fragments of my children
and now I am no longer human.

Now as every nation
seals its borders against us,
now as they gun us down
when we beg for sanctuary,
I will march America along
my tendons, electrify America
through my nerves.
Seal the borders of
my body to pain,
seal my eyes, mouth, belly
to any hunger not
my own.
I rename myself

America. No love

no grief in the world but mine.
And I will keep them safe –
in the cracks of my teeth
in the pit of my pelvis
in the raw raw flesh
beneath my eyelids.
Kamal
Gohar
Shahnaz
Sadiyah
Zainab
Zarafshan

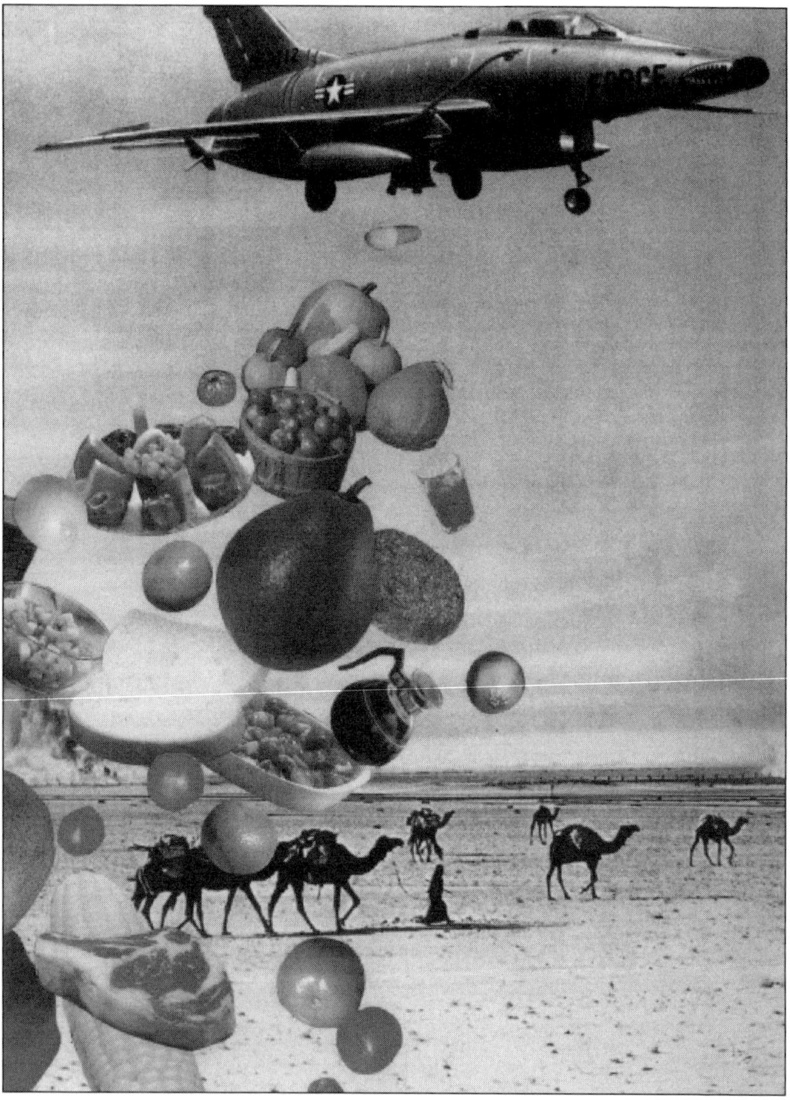
FORCE

Robert L. duRivage

Give Palestine Back To The Palestinians

No one in their own country should ever have to leave
just 'cause another country says so. That's not the way to be.
No one in their own country should ever have to fight
just to stay in their own country. It totally isn't right.

In Nineteen hundred and forty eight the U.S. made the call.
Give Israel to the Israelis- only Israelis one and all.
But that wasn't enough for them. They wanted a little more.
The Golan Heights and the Gaza Strip-Palestinians out the door.

I know the Jews have been kicked around all throughout history.
But that's not the way to handle things. That's not how it should be.
And if the U.S. keeps putting up with this, there's one thing that's for sure.
It's just the perfect recipe for a never-ending war.

Give Palestine back to the Palestinians!
Give Palestine back to the Palestinians!

We've got bigger things to worry about than attacking other lands.
Our air and water are poisonous. It's getting way out of hand.
If we don't make the right decision, if we don't do the right thing, their
won't be any more people to kick around. That song's way too sad to sing.

Give Palestine back to the Palestinians!
Give Palestine back to the Palestinians!
Give Palestine back to the Palestinians!
Give Palestine back to the Palestinians!

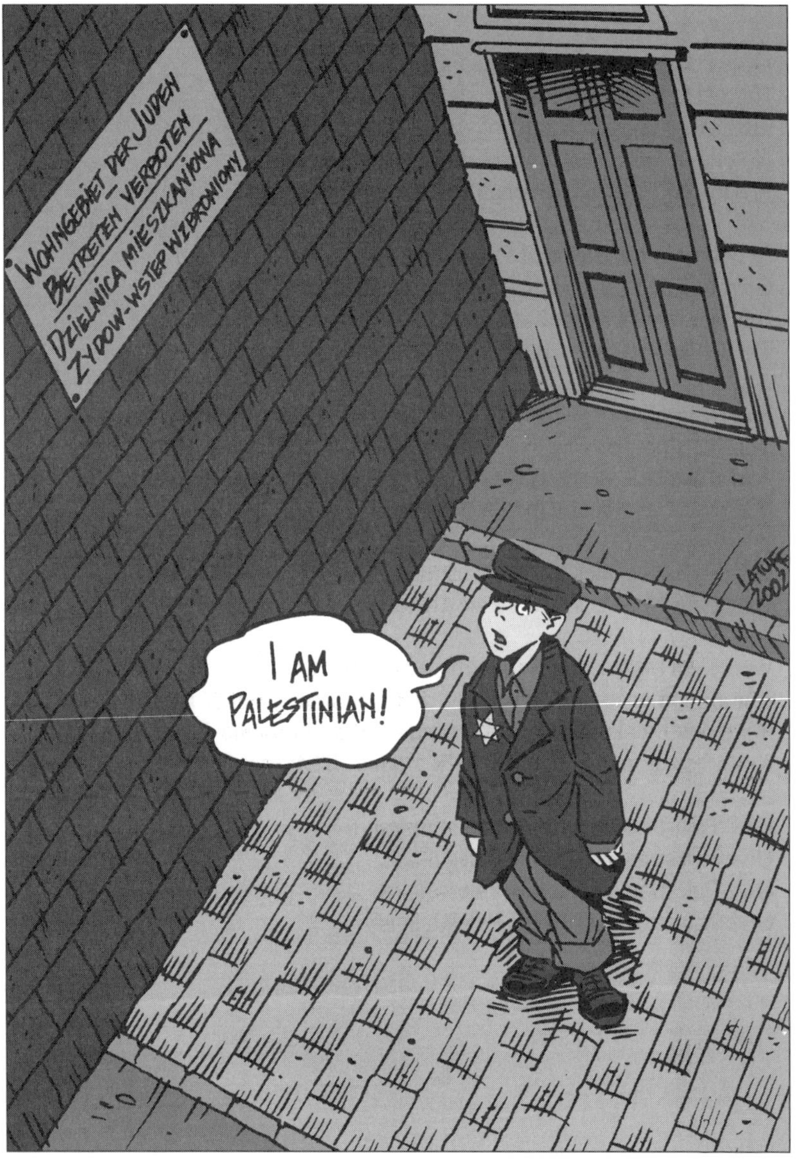
WOHNGEBIET DER JUDEN
BETRETEN VERBOTEN
DZIELNICA MIESZKANIOWA
ZYDOW-WSTEP WZBRONIONY
LATUFF 2002
I AM PALESTINIAN!

Ron Allen

Aboriginal Angst in the Key of Flow
The city-village of aboriginal angst
repressed fervor of exploded poetry
blue-black rythms of exploding steel funk
absolute funk of blood
blood of struggle
frozen in commerce
the mission of a transformed people
bleeding poems through the jembe
a mantra piercing walls of restraint
a single fist stops the bleeding heart
mission of sound
beating the ear with grief
speaking ink of tattoo frenzied fist
a fist-drum wired to wind
syncopated griot vein

Sound be warrior bell of freedom
sound be sex in midnight rebellion chant
ringing sweet as a walking 4/4
village of our minds
bone pole of future
walking tattoo of renaissance
oneless smoke of liberation
aboriginal crusade of knowledge
air of resistance
like dissin' death
like dissin' the shit of nations
like kissin' life full
of truth

Tattoo of capital
shallow steel sandwich of incarceration
spitting metal hate mushrooms
screams silent as whiskey

check, check physical beast of atonement
spike in the neck of America's joy
prison smoke house crack factory knowledge
splitting hairs of Buddha
kickin' ass and self-love flagellation
shroud of confinement
pre-shrunk T.V. consciousness
image of salt
totem of anger
peace, the joy of step
drum, drum renaissance time
drum-speak soup kitchen cadaver
aboriginal resist the mind and flesh
aboriginal resist the disrhythmia of colonialism

In the beginning there was sound
and it was without movement
and the movement was a word

deep piece of mystic / catalogue of spirit
sing song grip of patterned revolt
bottom of the word deep
inside the rhythm
aboriginal drum song slave revolt
bottom of the word deep
inside the rhythm
aboriginal drum song slave revolt
peace a jaw of primordial song
worn like missionary sex
colorized penis of blood
deep as rhythm

Drum preachin' tongue life rhythm
drum speakin' iron resistance
resist rigid faces of pus speak
scraping' the bottom for flavor
the city-village bottom of soul

money finger of tattoo lyric
the aboriginal check, check
matter to energy
energy to matter
mind speak drums speak
new time

Speak nature of fire tomorrow
prophecy of night spilling from lips
deep in red fire of aboriginal saints
pronouncement of justice
national jive of governments
perfume penitence of priests
mission of the fist
creating a new law of zeal
deep drum drama of tree and soil
drum speak time walking fist
arias and chants
speaking new blues
blues of octave drum riot time
change the riot of my nerves
inside rain cement
and iron fences

The tongue is a bullet rippin' lyric media passion time
speaking like the guru of kaleidascope dreams
round as moon time
chrysalis of nighthawk
absorbed as tree sap
deconstruction mirrors of square prophecies
in the city of rigid poverty
challenge the third eye to sight
prophecy of incantation
colors are whiskey-fed eyes
tattooed reptile skin
manhole-covered communion

Aboriginal lookin' for bullets
Lookin' for atonement
Lookin' for a new sky
Lookin' for sweetness in America
Lookin' for sentences hung in space

Mildewed words hung in space
dead as coyote
time as square holes in my lungs
in the city
the sound of rope resurrects truth
city of rigid poverty
resurrecting noise as sacrament
music to the jury of structure
rage in boxes of poverty
red as tattooed meaning
red as necktie police
red as dawn

Easy words of rebellion
kickin' big frame propaganda
checkin' the agents of void
measuring community as objects
of art
police glasses of time
severing our fists
city-village of now
wet words like sweat
walking griots of steel prisons
how do you treat aboriginal?

And the people said
And the people said
And the people said

And the people said
Amen.
Amen.
Amen-Ra.

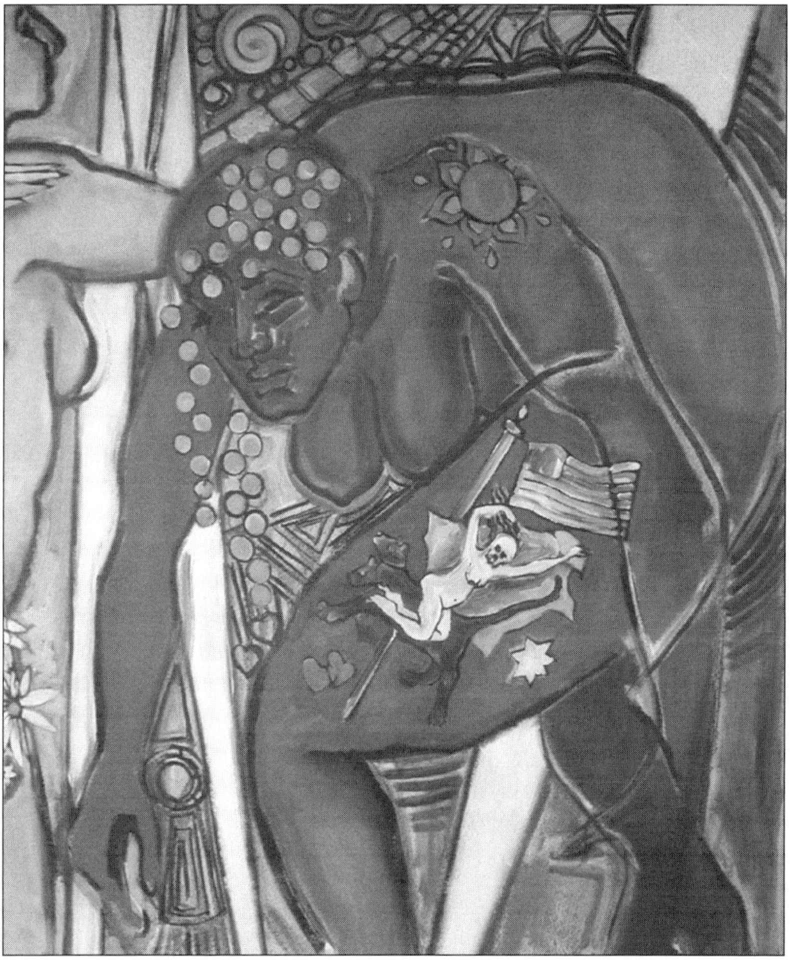

Andrea Geneste

MONKEYS WIELDED WEAPONS

monkeys wielded weapons
evolved in hypocrisy
and
genius was destroyed
canyons of carnage
from their mouths
neurological patriarchal dysfunction
speaks disaster
for the innocent

the power of the mind
seems to always come last
given to the sword
and warriors of past
reading between the lines
of their journalistic lies
i see they'd never die for me

is freedom a word they use
to mesmerize and entice
to tie our hands behinds our backs
as patriot heroes revered in song
and lead us through
a maze,
like blind mice
tying us in knots of nationalism
sending em up, flying in warplanes
waving symbols
of division
in the name of
in the name of nations,
in the name of religion
in the name of perspective
this miracle planet divided by land

this miracle planet divided by sea

this war is not chosen,
i couldn't kill
this war is not chosen,
no not by me

if i could build
build peace
if i could build
build, build, build

monkeys wield weapons
and evolve
in hypocrisy

POLICE THE WORLD
like they police our state
being caged seems to be our fate
evolution of woman and man
from jupiter's gate
limitless world
endless full moon glories
ended when the evils of control
blackballed the wiser stories
minds of destruction breed
eclipses to the soul
more hedonistic underneath
they'll surely pay the toll
they power trip
they've got a tight grip
or so they think
did they count it all up correctly
all those lives and earthly wonders
destroyed in the name of their
capitalistic pleasures

like little kids in battleship games
using humans as their tools
true glory blossoms
in those who disobey these rules
so how far off are you
on your once-beaten twice-beaten,
thrice-beaten path
do all the footprints before you
delight you with their math
did they all lead to happiness
in a materialistic world
with all those possessions
did it all add up to one plus two is three,
and let me ask you this
how is it gonna be
when you see me running
like a celestial primitive goddess out
of venus' water
towards the sun,
would you come along with me then?
would you run?

count it all up

why is all the glory we see in movies
why can't we experience it now
where is the romance in working
our bodies to the ground
where is the love in faking it
one more time
putting on the work face
just to make a dime
forgetting one more time
those people in the streets
who aren't just getting by
for tommorrow they may die

on a bench in the park
just another life going by
and meanwhile those on high
sit in plush plush rooms
with a cushion around their tomb
and you tell me this is freedom?
you tell me this is progress?

it's enough to make one mad
but i got enough love in me
to power up the general electric
cancer-infested megawatt world,
so you better watch out,
cuz here come the people
and this time you can't silence us
with pepper spray
this time you can't silence us
with conspiracy
innocent blood in the streets
under the guidance of police
defending their own,
or what they say that no one
 wants to hear in their
overnumbed, apathetic,
i work too long all day to care about
what goes on in the world,
oversimplified, sabotaged minds

center yourself in your world my friend
i'll see to it that your jupiter tree shall grow
and i shall center myself in mine
and as long as you bring peace my friend
we'll surely pick off purity
from that rebirthed jupiter vine

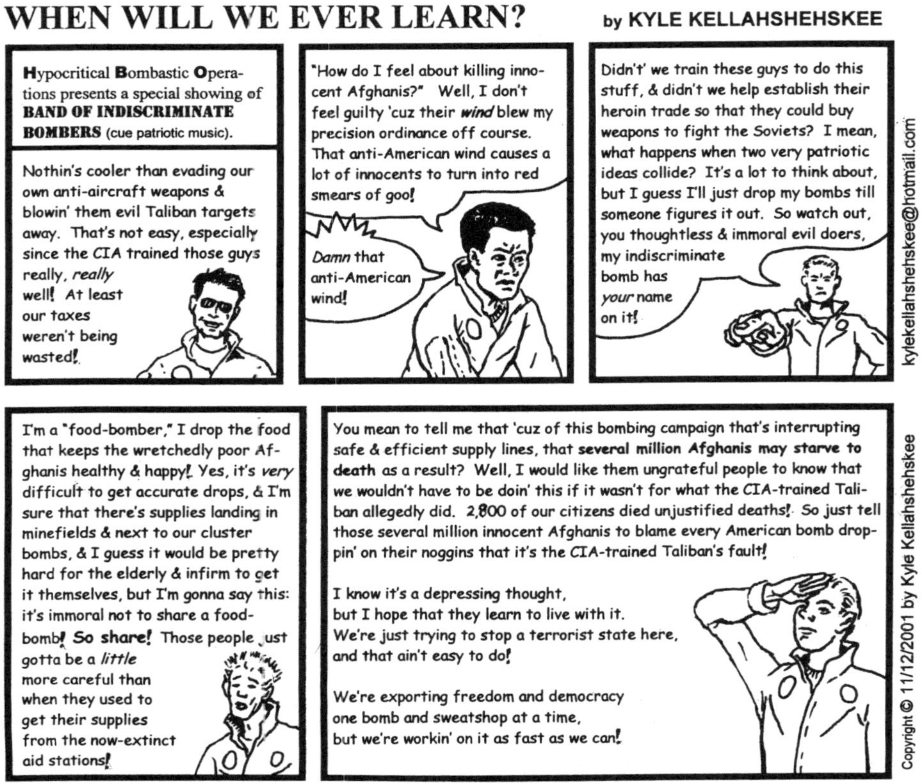
WHEN WILL WE EVER LEARN?
by KYLE KELLAHSHEHSKEE
Hypocritical Bombastic Operations presents a special showing of BAND OF INDISCRIMINATE BOMBERS (cue patriotic music).
Nothin's cooler than evading our own anti-aircraft weapons & blowin' them evil Taliban targets away. That's not easy, especially since the CIA trained those guys really, really well! At least our taxes weren't being wasted!
"How do I feel about killing innocent Afghanis?" Well, I don't feel guilty 'cuz their wind blew my precision ordinance off course. That anti-American wind causes a lot of innocents to turn into red smears of goo!
Damn that anti-American wind!
Didn't' we train these guys to do this stuff, & didn't we help establish their heroin trade so that they could buy weapons to fight the Soviets? I mean, what happens when two very patriotic ideas collide? It's a lot to think about, but I guess I'll just drop my bombs till someone figures it out. So watch out, you thoughtless & immoral evil doers, my indiscriminate bomb has your name on it!
kylekellahshehskee@hotmail.com
I'm a "food-bomber," I drop the food that keeps the wretchedly poor Afghanis healthy & happy! Yes, it's very difficult to get accurate drops, & I'm sure that there's supplies landing in minefields & next to our cluster bombs, & I guess it would be pretty hard for the elderly & infirm to get it themselves, but I'm gonna say this: it's immoral not to share a food-bomb! So share! Those people just gotta be a little more careful than when they used to get their supplies from the now-extinct aid stations!
You mean to tell me that 'cuz of this bombing campaign that's interrupting safe & efficient supply lines, that several million Afghanis may starve to death as a result? Well, I would like them ungrateful people to know that we wouldn't have to be doin' this if it wasn't for what the CIA-trained Taliban allegedly did. 2,800 of our citizens died unjustified deaths! So just tell those several million innocent Afghanis to blame every American bomb droppin' on their noggins that it's the CIA-trained Taliban's fault!
I know it's a depressing thought,
but I hope that they learn to live with it.
We're just trying to stop a terrorist state here,
and that ain't easy to do!
We're exporting freedom and democracy
one bomb and sweatshop at a time,
but we're workin' on it as fast as we can!
Copyright © 11/12/2001 by Kyle Kellahshehskee

William Copeland

Untitled

I'm not a pacifist
I'm not an activist
Still I call for peace "9-1-1"
is a joke like Flavor Flav told me
"Distasteful" so they call me
Public Enemy Number One—
          World
Public Enemy Number One—
          People
Public Enemy Number One—
          Organism We are
I call for Peace Speed Dial
Because I've committed suicide 5000
Times and nineteen more I've
Traded my center for the World of Illusions
And I'm Public Enemy Number One
Welcome to the Terrordome
as wiretaps metal detectors and interplanetary
tracking systems greet anxious citizens/employees
who sign social contracts
with spoiled brats
and sore losers for social security and safety
in numbers
The Earth is my mother
                    (sunuvabitch!)
My father was a bullet
                    (sunofagun!)
and everyday I explode
and everynight I explode   and everyday I explode
                                        and everynight I explode
and it's a new day
and the truth is you've probably been wasting a whole lotta time
and the truth is I've probably been wasting a whole lotta breath
lying to myself

like I'm not trying to kill myself
even as we speak
like I don't give away my powers to liberals and conservatives
authorities jurisdictions legislations
executions murders and attempted suicide
out of fear
coz something's off
out of fear
and we're too scared to look within to
find the truth
so we proceed and protest, rally riot and ruckus,
fuss and fidget
out of fear
one world
frustration
and I'm tired and sick
sick and tired
literally
Really I am healed and never died
I call for peace because my left hand knows not
What my right hand is doing
One organism
struggling to breathe
Bombs Over Baghdad
afraid of imagination
why are we
not taught
There must be another way:
Learn to love/
kill the messenger
One body
broken
but I will return
One blood
flowing
in the streets
nowadays

replenishing the soils
I shall rise
One organism
World's best kept secret
I AM
One being
Look past fears
One truth
Look to your neighbor
One world
It WILL happen
One reality
It can happen
One creation
Listen to your heart
as they say
it won't be televised
Recorded,
Reworded, placed on the course list
And taught at your universities
Human Being Access
One heart
leave here transformed
One word
not just entertainment
One peace
listening to the voice
One choice
as we say step out of fear
ONE LOVE.

Lynn Roman

Space

revolutions depend upon the gravity of the polar axis that we have to grind
and as we unwind, would you mind telling me how it is that the turn of the
world clicks to your time?
a time eternal need no paternal check work clock work boojie pop jerk
who integrates and postulates when statistically the next kid will die
when the next second will go by
when you finally earned the knowledge that you buy and buy
and by the way did he forget to say
when you should drop the bomb
five four three two
you won we lost
and was that second before your holocaust
the same length as that first curt kiss goodbye?
do you really think that moment, sent by a gravitational divine
equals the seconds on your chime
no, I fear your puppeteers must wind up, plug in and battery operate their
arms race
as your clocks turn and turn their revolutions are not born by an axis bent
but one with arms finely pulled across one dimension
perfectly balanced into obedience perfectly measured into equals —
or is it?
or does time always curve no matter who has the nerve to iron it flat
imagine that, rewind your watches, unhook your crotches, believe the
marches
this revolution has gotten its swing from people who are bent —
hell bent on reclaiming these dollars to make sense
not to feed the rich but for our true needs
expanding equality to account for inequalities
for the freedom to look inside ourselves
for every man woman and child to wake up and smile
at the trannies, animals, plants and grandparents
our revolutions begin to spiral
transcending time all the while

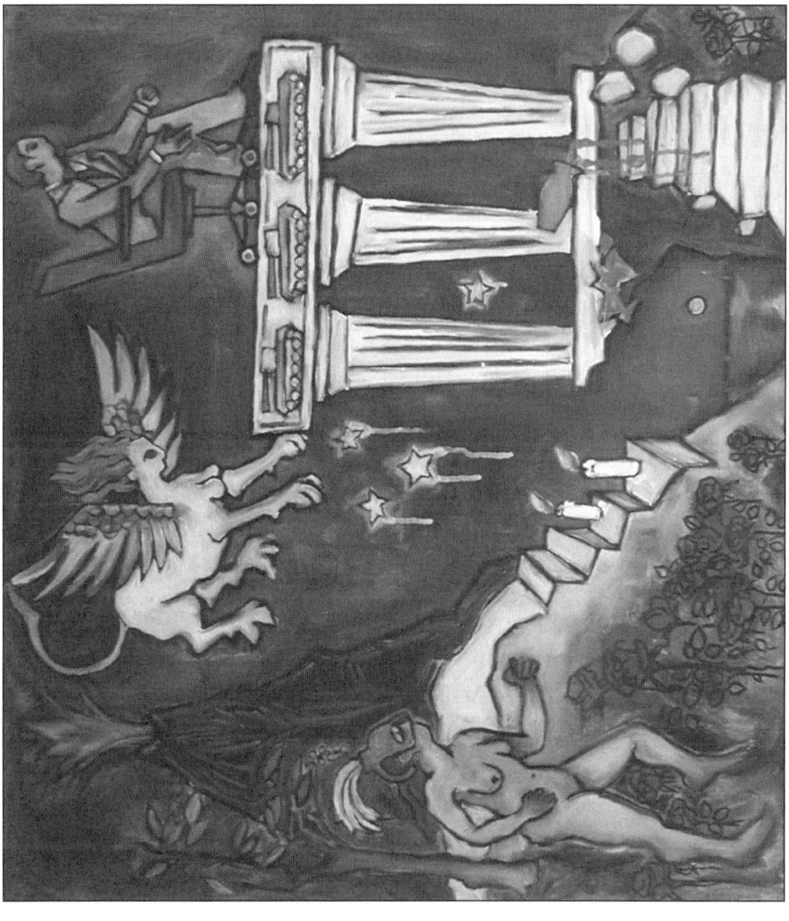

P.B. Brown

Untitled 1
You want to use me in your legions
You want me to fight your war
I have not experienced one of the things
That I am expected to give my life for

Freedom, Justice, Democracy, Fair play
Unfulfilled promises
Unfulfilled to this very day

Freedom has never been given the slave
Justice was rendered after entering the grave
As for the rest of those flowery words
Systematically denied by two wings, one bird

Untitled 2
Bigotry is her rabid dog
It's going to eat her up
She has suckled it and nurtured it
Since it was a rabid pup

Bigotry was never weaned from her
It still gnaws at her breasts
After bigotry has devoured her breasts
Bigotry will then devour the rest

Untitled 3
How can I think of Britannia
Without thinking of her daughter
Both have traversed the globe
Committing unspeakable slaughter

They have so much in common
Though they both have a different creed
The thing they have most in common

Is their voracious ravenous greed

Greed for gold, greed for diamonds
And an unhealthy desire to possess
Any and all natural resources
That are scarcely found in the west

They both have committed unspeakable slaughter
They both are extraordinarily mean
Her daughter commits murder for freedom and justice
Britannia, for the crown and the queen

Britannia wants here colonies back
She especially wants Iraq
To help her commit more unspeakable slaughter
She has enlisted the aid of her daughter

Britannia and her daughter
With their combined armed forces
Wish to re-acquire Iraq
And usurp her natural resources

If permitted to attack Iraq
Their greed will not decline
After Britannia has attacked Iraq
She will re-acquire Palestine

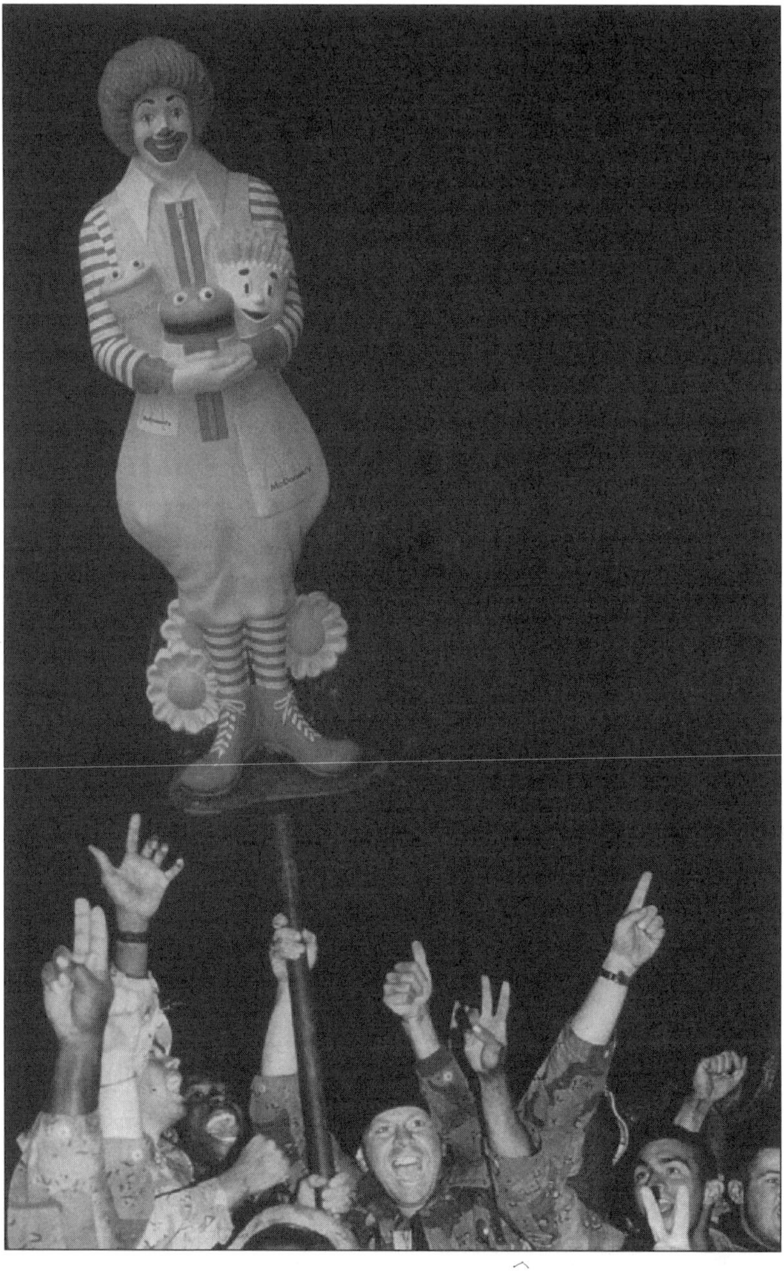

Jeff Shantz

Are we free yet?
The fearless battalions
Have knocked down the door
And boastful citizens
Don't talk so much anymore

Are we free yet?
Are we free yet?

Maniacal frat boys
Hold the whole world in their hands
And there's no one to stop them
Nobody to take a stand

Are we free yet?
Are we free yet?

The writing on the wall promises
Fortune and fame
But it's all we can do
To scream out our name

Are we free yet?
Are we free yet?

The smiles of the children
Have been wiped from their face
And only the dead
Recognize the disgrace

Are we free yet?
Are we free yet?
All of the bodies

Have been thrown in mass graves
And the President's speeches
Draw nothing but raves

Are we free yet?
Are we free yet?

When all of the mothers
Have gone home with their pain
Will anyone else speak
The cause of our shame?

Jessica R. Desjardins

Together as One
Total chaos, catastrophe.
Victims of violent tragedies.
Mourning souls, salvation stole,
through domination and control.
Reflect on us, and those who see
their beliefs are destroying humanity.
There was no time for them to breathe.
We must find time for us to grieve,
over the shadows of so many broken dreams.
Time heals all, so some say.
We must erase the horrors taken place.
As the heart begins to mend,
we must all come together as one.
United we all can put an end
to these acts of violence.

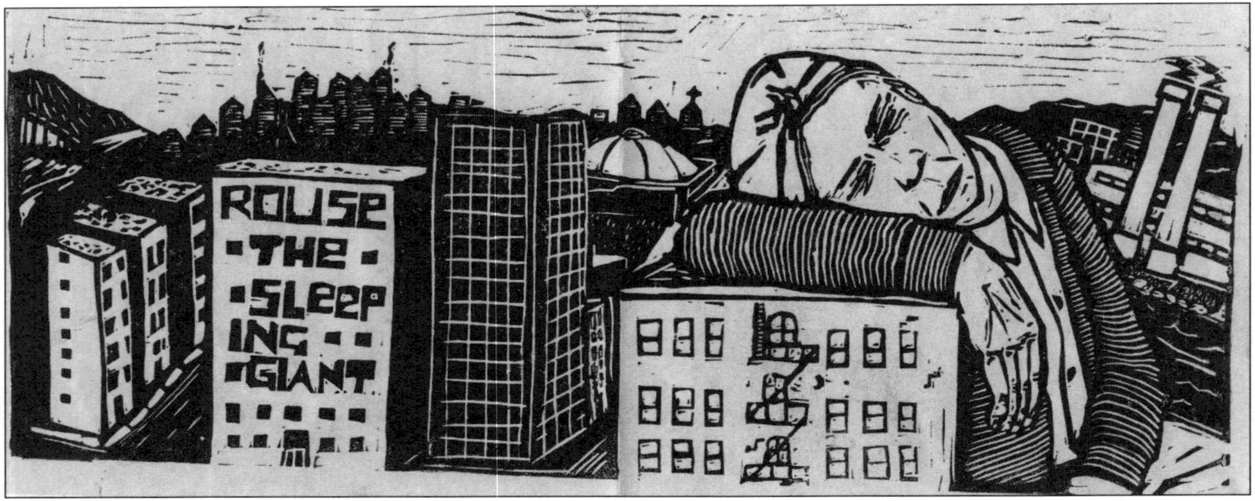
ROUSE THE SLEEPING GIANT

Joe Reilly

A Need for Healing
Slowly as we destroy the earth
our children watch
learning these ways.

Slowly as we destroy the earth
we destroy ourselves
and each other.

Making fun of the
way we need
water to live

Laughing at our
dependence on clean air
and water.

Slowly as we destroy the earth
our children
Who have not yet been born
cry
as we stuff money into their
mouths
to quiet them.

As if that would silence them.
As if that would keep them silent.

And here we are
insignificant and bare
following our egos into darkness.

Listen to the youth
listen to those

Whose creative connection
is still strong.

Let them lead us into the light
Let them lead us.

Slowly as we heal the earth
our parents watch
And remember these ways.

Slowly as we heal the earth
we heal ourselves
and each other.

Laughing at the way
water makes us free
and gives us hope.

Playing in pools of love
digging in the soil
-our Grandparents-

Slowly as we come together
in positivity
we heal the earth
we heal ourselves
we heal.

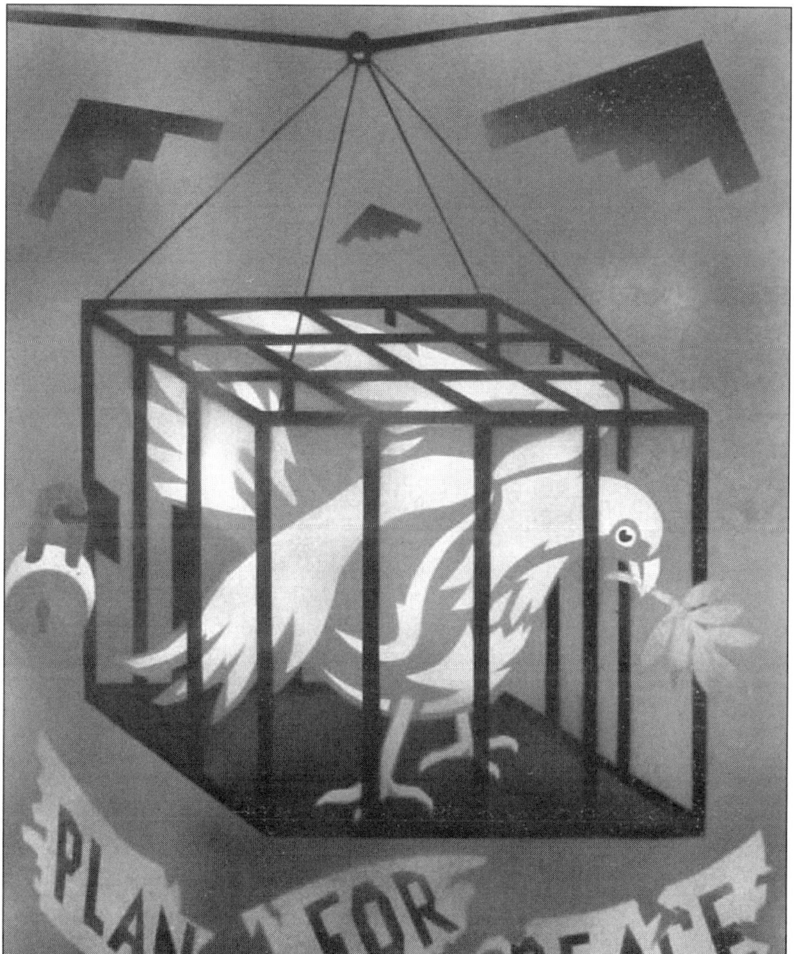
PLAN FOR PEACE

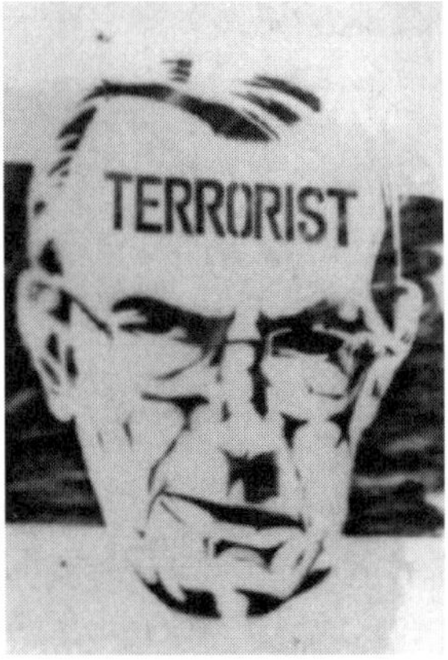

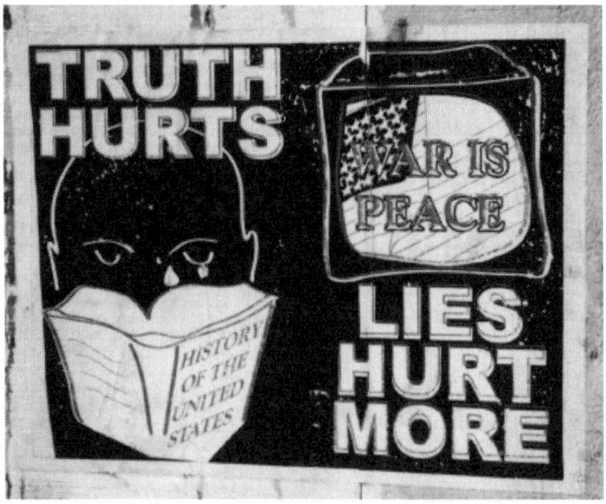

Under the weight of a million flags there is still the spark of discontent and resistance. September 11 created an intense chill on the public expression of dissent and disagreement with the government and status quo. We went from a strong and growing international revolt against global capitalism and a rebirth in local grassroots activism to what on surface looks like crushed and smothered shards of a movement. Although open dissent was effectively squashed, small gestures of disagreement and lack of faith in those in power are still creeping onto our landscape. These have been taking the form of graffiti, stickers, posters, and marker scrawls on walls across the country. These pages represent a small sampling of what the people that never make it into the mainstream media are saying about the state of the nation and the world.

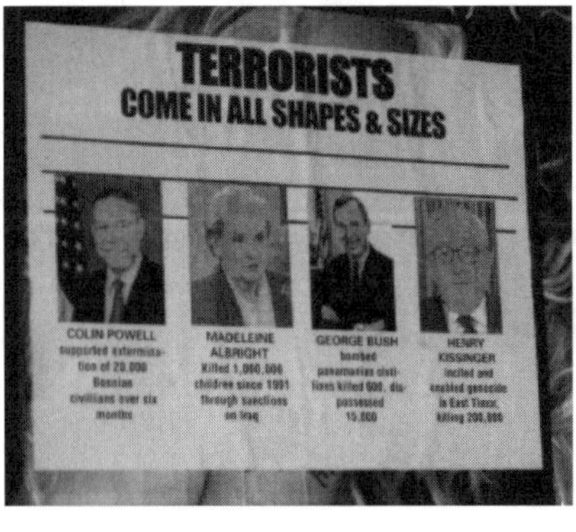

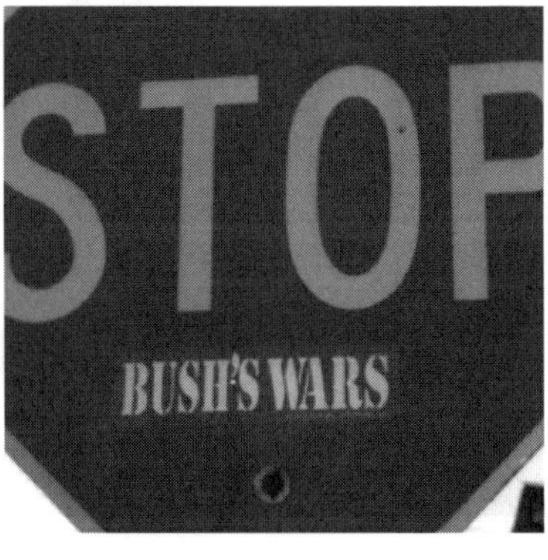

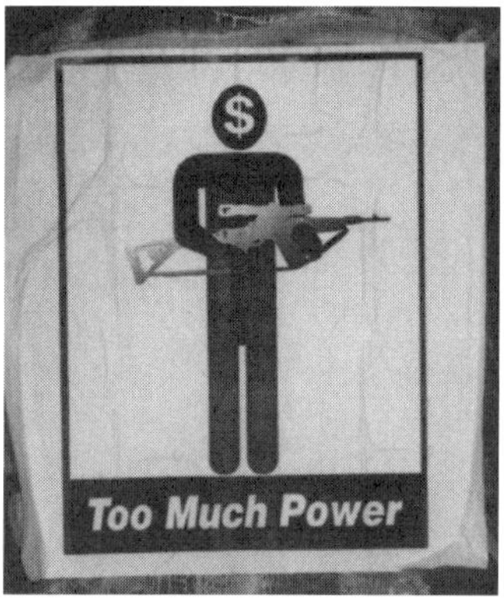
$
Too Much Power

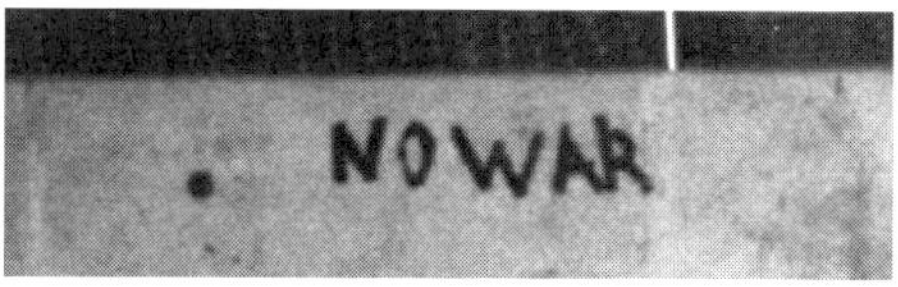
NO WAR

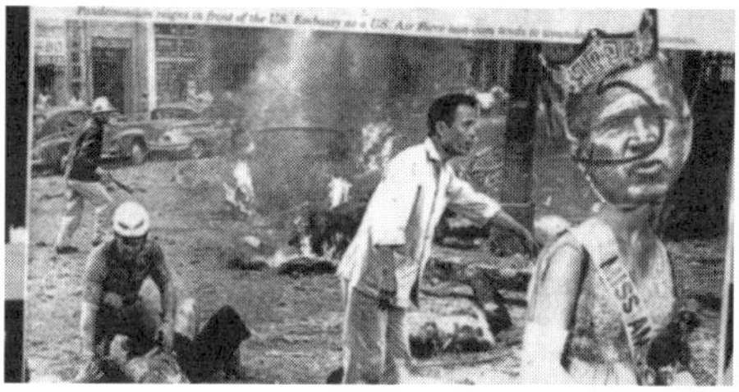

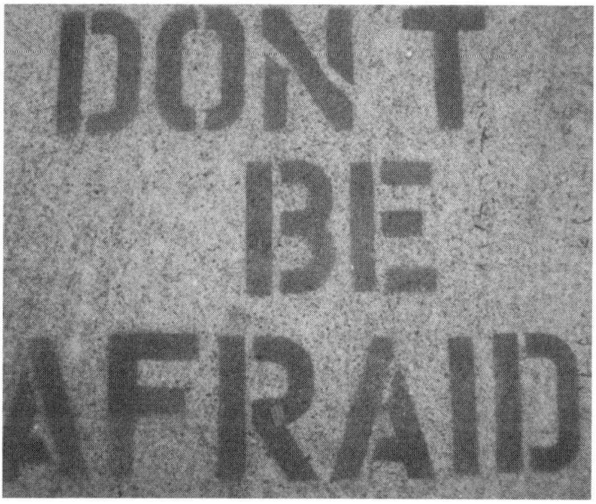
DON'T
BE
AFRAID

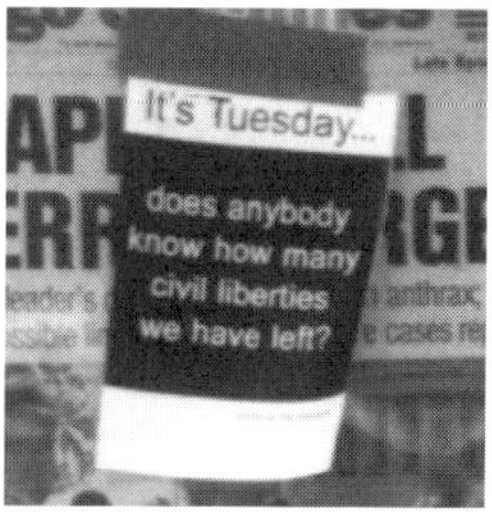
It's Tuesday...
does anybody know how many civil liberties we have left?

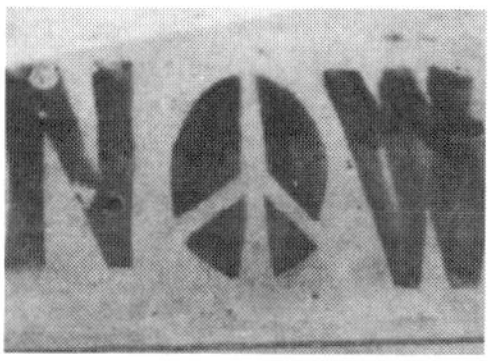
NOW

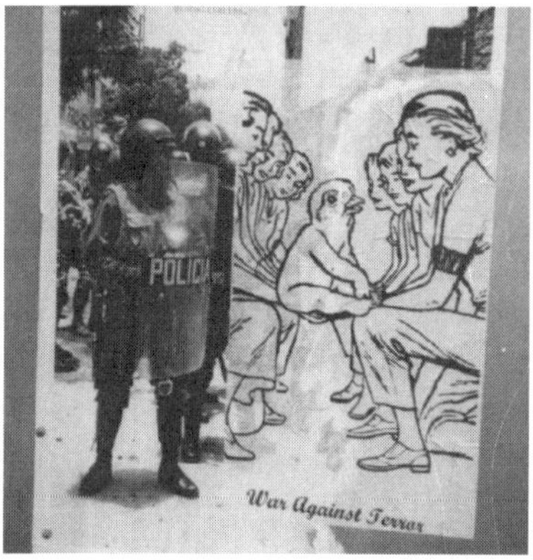
POLICIA
War Against Terror

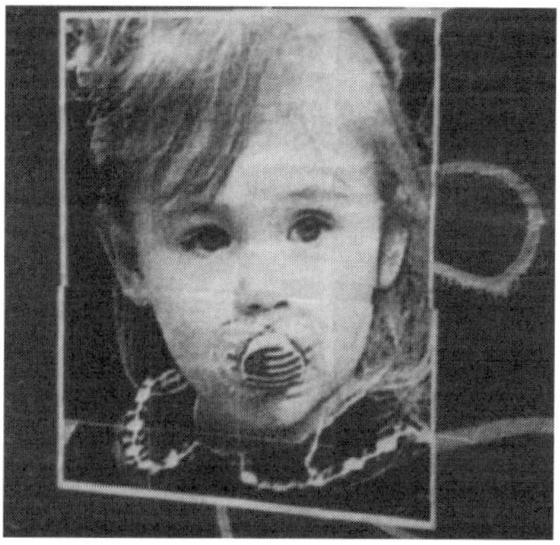

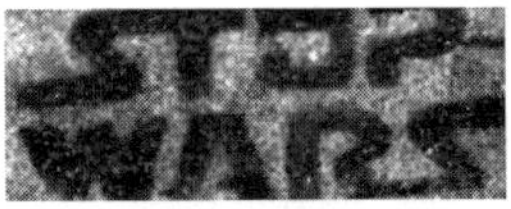
STOP
WARS

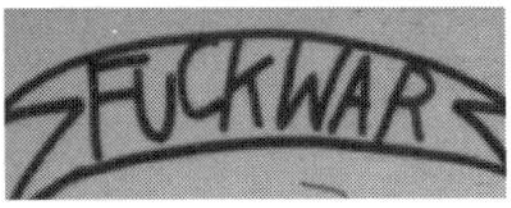
FUCK WAR

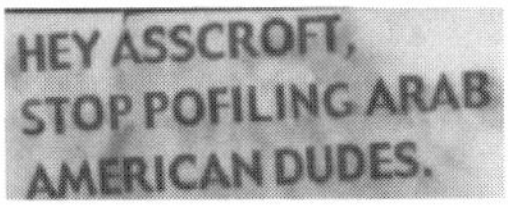
HEY ASSCROFT,
STOP POFILING ARAB
AMERICAN DUDES.

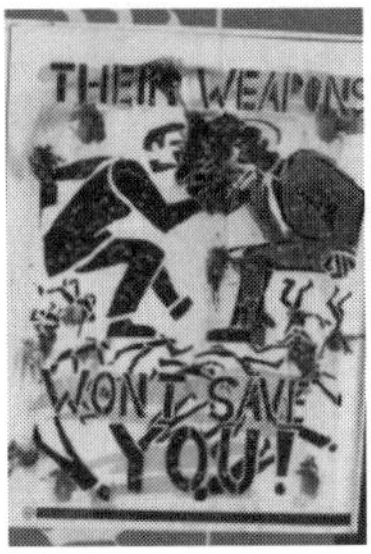
THEIR WEAPONS
WON'T SAVE
YOU!

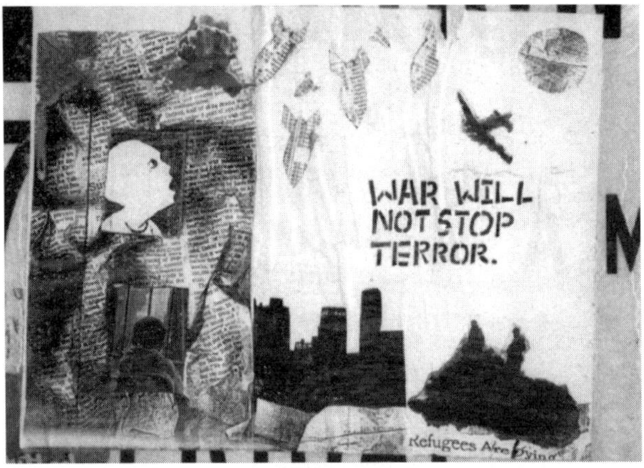
WAR WILL
NOT STOP
TERROR.

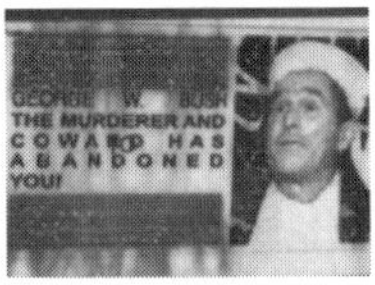
GEORGE W BUSH
THE MURDERER AND
COWARD HAS
ABANDONED
YOU!

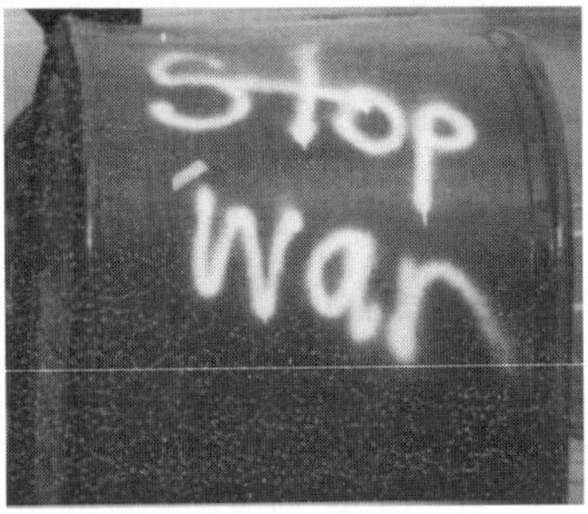
Stop
War

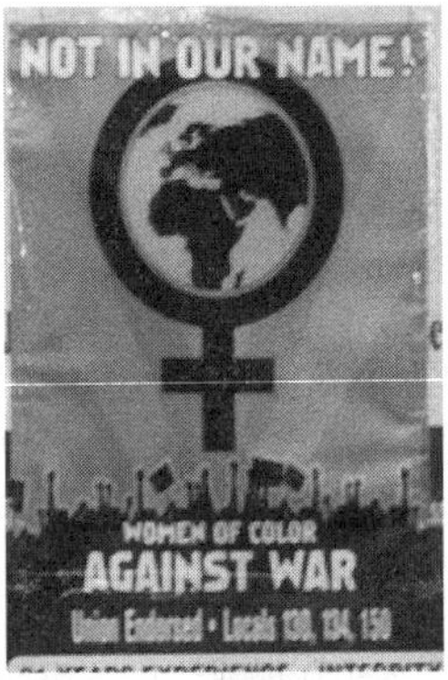
NOT IN OUR NAME!
WOMEN OF COLOR
AGAINST WAR
Union Endorsed • Locals 130, 134, 150

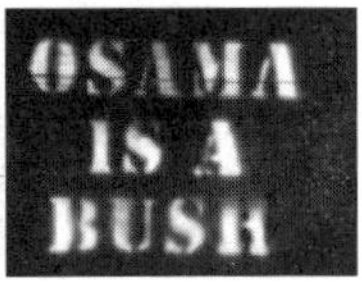
OSAMA
IS A
BUSH

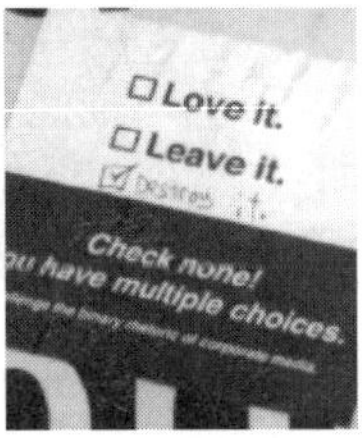
☐ Love it.
☐ Leave it.
☑ Destroy it.
Check none!
You have multiple choices.

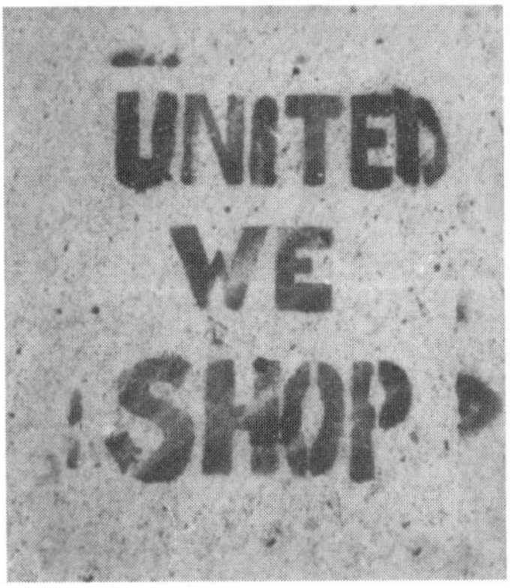
UNITED
WE
SHOP

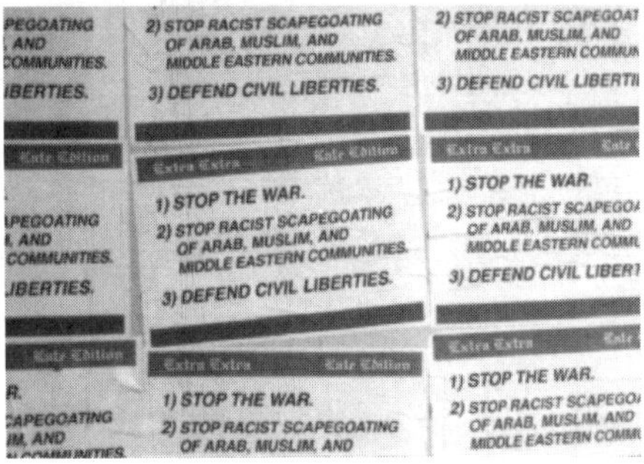
Extra Extra
Late Edition
1) STOP THE WAR.
2) STOP RACIST SCAPEGOATING OF ARAB, MUSLIM, AND MIDDLE EASTERN COMMUNITIES.
3) DEFEND CIVIL LIBERTIES.

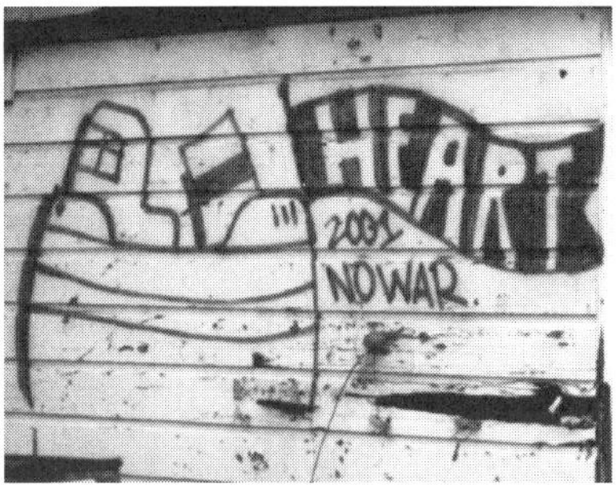

Credits: All artists anonymous unless otherwise noted; All photos/text by Josh MacPhee unless otherwise noted.

Page 1 (clockwise starting top left corner): Madison, WI, p: Miriam Hall; San Francisco; SF; Chicago.

Page 2: Chi.; Boston; Chi.; Chi.; SF; Chi., a: ATM; NYC; SF, p: Guenevere.

Page 3: SF; SF; Chi.; SF; NYC; Chi., a: United Culture & Troublemakers Union; Chi., a: UCTU; NYC; Chi.; Chi.; SF, a: Seth Tobocman; Chi.

This Page: Oakland; SF, a: Heart 101; Boston; Chi.; Chi.; Chi., a: Street Art Workers; SF, p: Russell H.

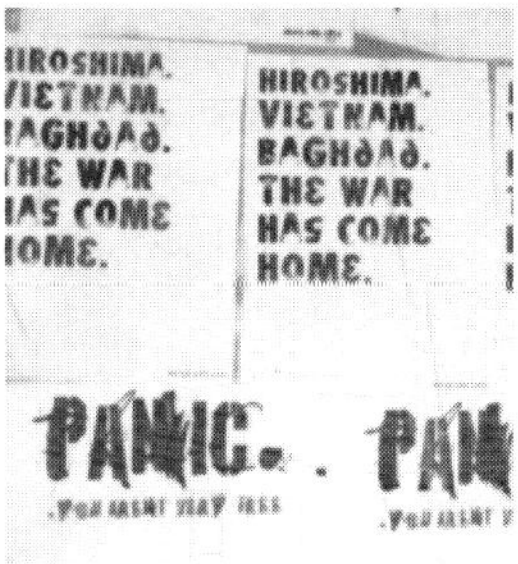

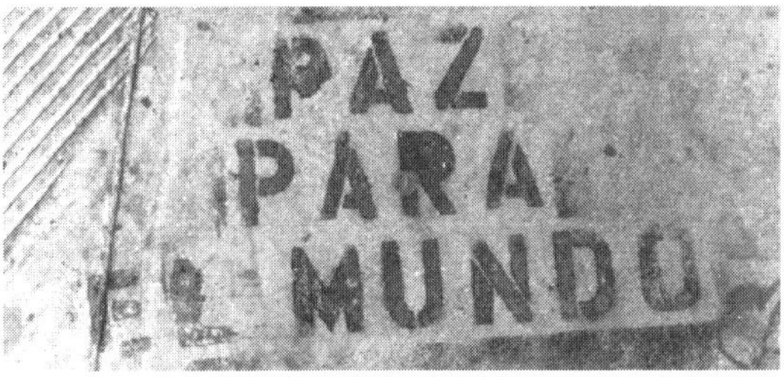

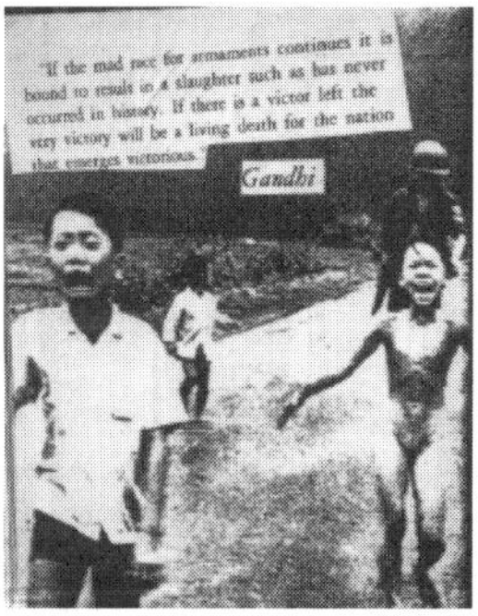

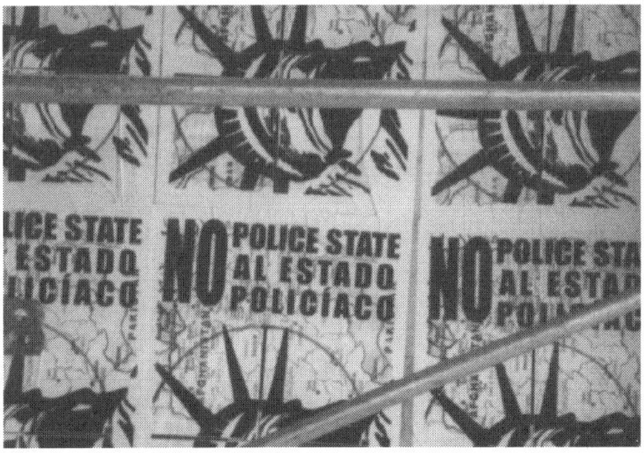

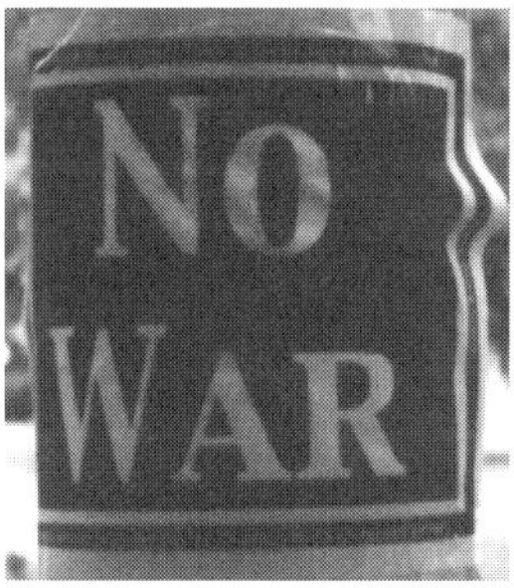

Upsidedown Culture Collective

TURN CULTURE UPSIDEDOWN: A statement of ideals

"By giving (the artist) privileged status, culture puts the artist in a position where (s)he can do no harm & in which (s)he functions as a safety-valve in the mechanism of bourgeois society." - The Atelier Populaire, Paris MAY '68.

Looking at one of the many definitions that can be found in the dictionary under the heading *culture*, we find "the training & refining of the mind, emotion, manners, taste, etc." This is culture as defined by the ruling class, the kind of culture only available to those w/ a fat bankroll & time on their hands. This is the sort of culture we want to turn on its head, to shake down or at the very least make irrelevant.

But there's been another kind of culture all along, running parallel to & struggling against this culture of death. This is the sort of culture we embrace—the culture of storytellers, musicians, writers, painters, farmers, thinkers who were above all else everyday people. Everyday people who realized that without considering all the world in their works of art (their lives) they were betraying themselves & others.

Drawing. Singing. Dancing. Playing. All these activities are important parts of life for young children, but as we grow up most of us stop engaging in them—we do so at our own peril.

We think that everyone has a creative part of their brain—distinct from the part of us that draws up blueprints or fills out tax forms. It is this part of our minds that keeps us connected to our dreams and emotions; our fantastic visions and our deepest needs.

We believe artistic projects and creative activities allow us to take guidance from this aspect of ourselves. To feel good. To break out of our mental prisons. To imagine new realities for the future. To give the culture of the ruling class a good, swift kick where it counts.

We stand for a culture of loud voices & laughter against silence & misery, a culture of togetherness & community against alienation, for green & growing things against concrete & asphalt, for adventure & experimentation —against dull acceptance & routine.

We stand for a culture that celebrates life & is in permanent revolution. We are fighting against a culture of death—capitalism & all the cold, hard things it prizes.

2. ART IS A WEAPON: FIGHT FOR LIFE

"There is no way to separate what I do as an artist from what I do as a human being... art is a weapon."- Paul Robeson.

We seek to infuse popular struggles with creative energy. This means experimenting with how we interact with each other, spread ideas, and work on constructive projects to transform the world around us. We believe more people will participate in efforts to improve our lives when our activities are engaging and create moments of time that push beyond the boundaries of our usual experiences.

We also believe the active participation of many people is central to creating meaningful change. We do not believe in master plans. Everyone should be involved in helping shape the projects we choose to work on in our own individual ways. Everyone should be given an opportunity to develop our own personal visions for the future. After all, we believe our own lives are the most important creative outlet we have.

We hope that empathy and understanding for other people will spring out of the emotional bonds created by creative action, allowing us to improve our communication and problem-solving skills and to decrease our violence and animosity towards one another.

We feel that all to often people engaged in creative activities fail to take responsibility for the unpleasant realities of the world around us.

We are actively demanding that people use their vision and imagination to draw attention to larger patterns that keep folks down, to help transform our world for the better, to make people feel good and give us courage and hope. We also want to let artists know that we find producing art solely to please wealthy patrons and to make money to be sick, sick, sick.

3. WHAT WE WANT & WHY WE SAY IT SO LOUDLY

Upsidedown Culture Collective wants to help create a world worth getting excited about when we wake up in the morning! We believe collective creative action is the way to get there!

We're looking for:

A world supercharged by creative energy!
A world where our basic material and emotional needs are met!
A world where we do with our bodies as we please!
A world of possibilities!
We will not just settle for less suffering!
Joy, dignity, freedom will be our watchwords!
A world not forced upon us by reckless power!
A world where violence is not seen as normal!
A world of danger, perhaps, but not of constant menace and confusion!
A world where we are not scared of one another!
A world where the numbness is gone!
A WORLD TRANSFORMED!
More laughter, scribbling, dancing and by all means music!
More touching!
More movement for the muscles of our bodies!
More romance and wild adventures!
More of the unknown and unexpected!
A world of closer, deeper relationships with
Each other
Ourselves
The world around us!
A world where we dare!
Brought about by what WE do today!

Upsidedown Culture Collective

Resources we recommend

It's obvious the calm, authoritative voices that greet us on our TV sets and in our newspapers are more concerned about updating us about the world's problems than doing anything about them. Here are some sources of information and inspiration we recommend you check out.

With so many resources to share in 2003, United States of America, especially with all the new information online, a comprehensive list would be a book in itself. This list is far from complete, and we realize that it does not even touch upon many subjects or ways to learn more. We also suggest you use your local libraries as a resource and hopefully there you will find computers to access some of these sites and real people to talk to.

AK Press Distribution - One way to find some of the aforementioned book titles, and more. Look online at *www.akpress.org* or write for a free catalogue at 674-A 23rd St. Oakland, CA 94612.

Left Bank Books - Another great distributor of books and more. 92 Pike St.-Box B Seattle, WA 98101; *www.leftbankbooks.com.*

www.100fires.com - Website of extraordinary books (and more) for a healthy planet

www.indymedia.org - The news corporate America will not allow.

www.znet.org - Online edition of news from this magazine, which is found in most Borders etc.; if not, ask them to stock it.

www.war-times.org - "First casualty of war is truth." Website and tabloid size newspaper for the peace and justice movement and those interested in learning more.

9-11 by Noam Chomsky - MIT linguist, and one of the most influential and intellectual of authors concerned with US foreign and domestic policies genuine effects on our world. His thoughts on the September 11th, 2001 attacks are important and thought provoking. *Seven Stories Publishing.*

www.beehivedesigncollective.org - A great example of using art to break down barriers & communicate radical messages. They are a political graphics workshop that creates narrative posters out of interviews, with the collaboration of many organizers, and teach people a trade via a mosaic mural apprenticeship! Write to them at 3 Elm St. Machias, Maine 04654.

The Cartoon History of the Universe (3 volumes) by Larry Gonick - A comprehensive history of, well, the universe. Incredibly funny, well-researched, and informative. An easy way for folks to get an understanding of history that can put our present in a little perspective. *Doubleday Books.*

Introducing... series - An excellent series of books available at many bookstores that breaks down ideas about philosophy, sociology, psychology and cultural studies by using pictures and comics. A very readable way to get familiar with ideas that can be put into practice for social change. *Icon Books.*

Poetry in revolt, website - An archive of Anarchist and Radical Poets. You might be suprised who you find here: William Blake, Ralph Waldo Emerson, Diane Di Prima, Carl Sandburg. A good resource to get a feeling for the long and enduring link between poetry and radical change. *www.angelfire.com/mn2/anarchist poetry.*

Clamor, magazine - A bimonthly magazine offering new perspectives on politics, culture, media and life. Provides a media outlet that reflects reality, alternative culture and politics in a format that is accessible to and readable. P.O. Box 1225, Bowling Green Ohio 43402; *www.clamormagazine.org*.

AWOL Magazine, Revolutionary Artists Workshop (includes spoken word and hip hop cd) - Packed with art, interviews and articles from marginalized voices it is critical we all read and listen. 1515 Cherry St. Philadelphia, PA 19102; 1-800-NO-JROTC; *awol.objector.org.*

The Dispossessed by Ursula K. Leguin - A science-fiction novel that provokes challenging thought on both utopias & societies based on property ownership, laws and government.

World War III Illustrated, magazine - A magazine devoted to reporting and expressing political ideas through comics since 1980. Check it out at a newsstand near you. P.O. Box 20777 Tompkins Square Station New York, NY 10008.

www.art-for-a-change.com - Political/punk artist Mark Vollen's site has an excellent radical art history section.

www.rtmark.com - Tons of "market driven", smart and often simple pranks, that mean to hurt the system that so hurts people. Lots of ideas and inspiration here!

Feminist Theory: From the Margin to the Center by bell hooks - A great challenging book from an important feminist thinker. *South End Press.*

Memory of Fire trilogy by Eduardo Galeano - A poetic, subjective and breathtaking retelling of Latin & Native American history. *Norton Publishing.*

A People's History of the United States by Howard Zinn - Essential Reading. *Harper Perrenial.*

Gender Outlaw by Kate Bornstein - Essential Reading. *Vintage Books.*

www.adamah.org - One attempt at a practical vision of utopia in Detroit.

www.dsni.org - Once upon a time there was a Boston neighborhood in distress and the people living there did something about it, really did something about it! Great source of inspiration for those ready to take back control of their neighborhoods, and lives.

www.palsolidarity.org - "a Palestinian-led movement of activists" working to have awareness of the struggle for Palestinian freedom & an end to Israeli occupation.

The SUN: a magazine of ideas - Isn't political, literary or spiritual in the usual sense. Stories, articles, photography and poetry on… life, submitted by its readers. *www.thesunmagazine.org.*

The Creation of Patriarchy by Gerda Lerner - An intense & well researched historical look at the origins of the collective dominance of women by men. *Oxford Press.*

Crimes of War: What the Public Should Know - Meant as a field guide for journalists covering conflicts and wars in the world, before the phenomenon of "embedded journalists", it is an excellent guide to the ins and outs of the worst humanity has to offer. *W.W. Norton & Company*.

What IF?: Journal of Radical Possibilites - Two volumes (thus far) of pure inspiration and imagination, articles, art, history and radical vision. 125 Buena Vista Terrace San Francisco, CA, 94117.

Indian Givers: How the Indians of the Americas Transformed the World by Jack Weatherford - Stories of all the many contributions that have been ignored and underrated, taken from American Indians, or learned from them. From capitalism to anarchism, to the culinary, agricultural & industrial revolutions and much more.

The Surrealist Movement in the United States, website - Radically different from other websites "about" surrealism—the great majority of which contain nothing but misinformation —this site is the voice of the Surrealist Movement itself. They believe, surrealism was—and still is—the most thorough going expression of individual revolt and social/cultural revolution. P. O. Box 6424, Evanston, IL 60204; *www.surrealism-usa.org.*

They Live (1988), movie - Director John Carpenter's classic movie about aliens who appear human and use advertising and subliminal messages to make humans numb to the rising poverty, joblessness, environmental destruction and social collapse that is destroying humanity and the planet. A fantastic example of how imagination can be used to make complex ideas intelligible.

Prison Activist Resource Center - Striving for a society in which prisons would not be needed and could not be justified, this group provides support for educators, activists, prisoners and prisoner's families. P.O. Box 339 Berkley, CA 94701. *www.prisonactivst.org.*

www.jewsagainsttheoccupation.com - An organization of proggresive, secular, & religious Jews of all ages throughout the New York City area advocating peace through justice for Palestine and Israel. Includes current events, resources and information about the group.

Salt of the Earth (1953), movie - Film about striking Chicano and Anglo miners and their families. In the film the miners played themselves and it was made on site. The crew was made up of blacklisted technicians, and only two professional actors appear in it. A masterpiece!

www.pneumabooks.com - Your publishing questions answered. (if only we had known).